PRAISE FOR THE ARCHITECT OF OIKOS

Within the pages of *The Architect of Oikos* Angela Broussard captures and carries the sound of the power of that which is authentically kingdom. Not only does she write deeply on the subject, she passionately lives the reality of what she writes. You can hear in Angela, and in her writing, an "aged" sound, because she is not introducing new things, as many often attempt, but something that is foundational, aged, tried, and tested. This not only clearly indicates the stature of the writer, but also the heart behind the words she pens. She is what she writes. This is not very common today, unfortunately. Today, we suffer from too many words coming out of hearts that are often too little. Not here. The opposite is true in this case, there are too few words in this book, but thankfully, there are many more in the heart of the author. We can only hope that the heart keeps pumping, and the words keep forming. Within Angela, a beautiful and glorious unfolding is taking each of us on a journey to a destination that may exist as concept in our minds, but one that is extraordinarily difficult to find in life. Angela can help us get there, and I, for one, and am ready to go.

— DR JOSHUA TODD, PRESIDENT, KINGDOM
LEADERSHIP INSTITUTE & AUTHOR *SEASONS OF
SONSHIP* SERIES *PURIFIED POWER* SERIES
WWW.DRJOSHUATODD.COM

The author has a masterful grasp of the Word of God and also of the English language. The words she uses to craft this story grabs you the reader from the first paragraph and holds you captivated throughout the book. It tells of a chasm brought about by the deception of the deceiver, Satan; a plan by the Father for bridging the divide; and the sacrifice of Christ our Redeemer to repair the breach and restore fallen humanity to a position of trust.

This is one book that all seekers of truth will want in your library and one you will read and reference frequently. Angela, thanks for writing another inspired book that uncovers the plot of the evil one while highlighting the redemptive love and sacrifice of Christ.

— ELVIE GUTHRIE-LEWIS, AUTHOR OF *WARM REGARDS: INSPIRATION 365*; INTERNATIONAL SPEAKER; WELLNESS & GRATITUDE COACH; AND PRESIDENT OF GUTHRIE & GUTHRIE CONSULTING

THE ARCHITECT OF OIKOS & THE BLUEPRINTS OF KINGDOM CULTURE

ALSO BY ANGELA BROUSSARD

Doors Gates & Threshold Series Book 1:

The Name Speaks

THE ARCHITECT OF OIKOS & THE BLUEPRINTS OF KINGDOM CULTURE

REPAIRING THE BREACH IN THE HOUSE OF GOD
IN THE ERA OF REFORMATION

ANGELA BROUSSARD

Foreword by
REBECCA D BENNETT

3 TREES

Repairer of the Breach
You chose to repair the Foundation of Firsts.
You are my Cornerstone; and my Honeycomb Scroll.
I return to You this work as a revelatory talent.
May all the families of the earth be blessed
as the increase expands Your domain
in the understanding of Your
people.

The Architect of Oikos & The Blueprints of Kingdom Culture: *Repairing The Breach In The House Of God In The Era of Reformation,* Doors Gates Thresholds Series Book 2

Copyright © 2022 by Angela Broussard

www.silvercornerstone.com

angela@silvercornerstone.com

3Trees Publishing, 18024 Dedeaux Clan Road, Gulfport, MS 39503

3TreesPublishing@gmail.com

ISBN: 979-8-9860289-8-9 print

ISBN: 979-8-9860289-9-6 ebook

LCCN: 2022912618

Cover Design: Laura Rivera-Rexach contact@designsxlaura.com

Editor: Heidi Cook heidi@heidicookstudios.com

Graphic: Copyright 2017 Faithlife / Logos Bible Software

CONTENTS

FOREWORD

REBECCA D BENNETT

Often times our identity remains rooted in traumas and negative experiences that hinder our spiritual development and maturation. It causes our purpose to linger in a state of idleness. We wander further and farther from our original intent as it was spoken before the foundations of the earth. When the turbulent seas of experiential chaos and the miles of demon-filled wilderness carry us to the depths of our very own soul leaving us to exist alone, naked, hungry and afraid, how shall we respond? King David responded like this in the Book of Psalm 42:4-8, The Passion Translation:

So I speak over my heartbroken soul, "Take courage. Remember when you used to be right out front leading the procession of praise when the great crowd of worshippers gathered to go into the presence of the Lord? You shouted with joy as the sound of passionate celebration filled the air and the joyous multitude of lovers honored the feast of the Lord!" So then, my soul, why would you be depressed? Why would you sink into despair? Just keep hoping and waiting on God, your Savior. For no matter what, I will still sing with praise, for you are my saving grace! Here I am depressed and downcast. Yet I will still remember you as I ponder this place where your glory streams down from the mighty mountaintops, lofty and majestic— the mountains of your awesome presence. My deep need calls out to the deep kindness of your love. ...All through the day Yahweh has commanded his endless love to pour over me.

How do we arrive at such a place of understanding? It begins through the reading of God's Word and by having a personal relationship with him through the redemption of his Son, Jesus. It is by his Spirit we learn the marvelous treasures and mysteries of His Kingdom. The Book of Job 28:23-28, The Message Translation, puts it this way:

God alone knows the way to Wisdom; he knows the exact place to find it. He knows where everything is on earth, he sees everything under heaven. After he commanded the winds to blow and measured out the waters, arranged for the rain and set off explosions of thunder and lightning, he focused on Wisdom, made sure it was all set and tested and ready. Then he addressed the human race: "Here it is! Fear-of-the-Lord--that's Wisdom, and Insight means shunning evil."

We come to know Wisdom through the Fear of the Lord, and insight comes from shunning evil. When we pursue relationship with God and learn to resist the wilderness, we gain Wisdom and Insight. Therefore, who shall teach Knowledge? Righteous and just Knowledge come from the Lord. Those worthy to teach on his behalf have marinated the meat of the Word in the Fear of the Lord. They fully experience the revelation of Truth found in his Word. When the scriptures have developed within a person to move beyond mere words formed from precept to concept and become the character forming behaviors and habits that make up the very nature and image of God in the earth, just as Jesus and the Apostles did over two thousand years ago, they have found Wisdom. They are worthy to teach others, so they too may come to know Wisdom.

What will confront and challenge your Biblical intellect? Those things that cause you to question, "What is line upon line, and precept upon precept?." This is one such book! *The Architect of Oikos & The Blueprints of Kingdom Culture* comes from such a place of deep revelation of God's Word marinated in Wisdom. Angela Broussard has masterfully written about the construct of God's original intent through each of our lives which build and expand a Kingdom, utilizing the element of humanity. We are mere clay vessels formed to construct His house and yet we are each our own formed in Him.

Humanity began for the expansion of the Kingdom of God. Life trials attempt to cause us to forget why we are and what we are to do. The *Architect of Oikos & The Blueprints of Kingdom Culture* allows one to align their identity, regardless of its present condition, with God's original intent and build upon the solid foundation provided through Jesus so that one's purpose may begin moving out of an unproductive state for the benefit of personal and Kingdom fulfillment.

It has been an honor to know someone who will challenge those things that we think we know. Angela does just that. "Iron sharpens iron!" she often remarks. That has been the sort of friendship that has evolved over the years. Our friendship is the kind where we 'study to show ourselves approved.' To others, she is an amazing teacher, prayer warrior, and exhorter. To me, she is so much more. You will come to know and love her just as so many others have through her words, her teachings, and her uncompromised love for Truth. Thank you, Angela, for your labor of love. Truly you are a living demonstration of one living within the Oikos of the Kingdom.

Rebecca D Bennett
Author, *The Destiny Series*
Executive Director & Co-Founder
Wells of SouthGate
Entrepreneur/Business Owner/Change Agent
www.rebeccadbennett.com

INTRODUCTION

I hail from a family of pioneers.

Arriving in America late 1727, my paternal generations had left behind the ravishes of war torn Germany, wearied from the clash and deep scars of political and religious tensions foisted upon them during the Thirty Years War. They came with the knowledge that they would establish community upon the cultural value system found in Scripture. Alighting upon a bucolic North Carolina hill, my family established a place of worship, still in use today.

Settling in included building houses in which families could dwell; a milling center for commerce; a voting precinct to establish governmental matters; and a community center as a public gathering place for social and civic affairs. In addition to spiritual guidance, those of my lineage invested in the education of the community in numerous ways, providing and producing statured leaders to guide the prosperity of those in proximity. Writing of my forebears, William Whitsett wrote:

> "All these local settlers had come ... and by frequent intermarriages wove the ties of family and church life into firm bands. Without

exaggeration it may be claimed for them that they were liberty-loving and God-fearing people."[1]

My ancestors understood the basic building blocks necessary to develop sustainable growth among a people group. Continuing his premise, William Whitsett quoted English orator Dr. Robert Hall:

"Families are so many centers of attraction, which preserve mankind from being scattered and dissipated by the repulsive powers of selfishness."

"... so in the development of the passions, in like manner, we advance from private to public affections; from the love of parents, brothers, and sisters, to those more expanded regards which embrace the immense society of human kind." - Dr. Robert Hall

The foundations my forefathers laid were established upon upright spiritual principles, and provided the framework of a society prepared to carry the weight of continuity for generations. This was the condition in which I discovered the two courageous brothers of 1727. They were steeped in the covenant principles of faith and family, and willingly traversed the ocean to forge community anew. Yet, one pioneering generation begets another pioneering generation. From their loins came others with bold, pioneering tendencies, who explored and established, in varying degrees of expression, based on circumstance and Providence.

Pioneering is an inborn trait that launches explorers and change agents. When pioneers pursue the unknown from the base camp of sustained cultural security, they carry with them the fortitude supplied by the maturing components of a stable environment. New horizons of trade and exchange occur, and ultimately, a destination is reached wherein a new outpost crops up in the landscape of life. A fresh community emerges, a culture is established, and the process begins again. The pioneers birthed from cultural stability arrive at a destination and germinate the new from the seedbed of the former.

In other scenarios, where cultural standards have been breached or broken at a covenant level, a pioneer may embark on a soul-searching quest for adventure, driven by a deep-seated longing to discover the unexplainable, intangible experience of stability unknown to them. When the pioneers of this cloth strike out, they tend to decry the need for community and culture. Instead, they glory in their ability to maneuver in the wild, honoring rugged independence above the anchoring effect of a stable society. These represent a noble cause, yet due to the aforementioned broken covenant principles, the capacity to produce long-term social stability becomes the missing link of their powerful efforts. Nomadic in their pursuit, trails are blazed and temporary outposts created, but an unsustainable way of life is exposed. Healthy cultural norms and boundaries are lacking, driving broken relationships and broken dreams. Scattered families, a symptom of broken covenant, emerge.

The kingdom of darkness works willingly with this principle of scattering, listed in Deuteronomy as a curse for disobedience to the God of creation. The forces set against the Kingdom of God use division and isolation to their benefit, as a distraction, while they surreptitiously build another structure out of the *'repulsive powers of selfishness.'* These strongholds resist the knowledge of God, and push humanity off-course, far from the stabilizing influence of the King.

As a result, the pillars of marriage and family, from which all other pillars of Kingdom culture are produced, have experienced disrepair and damage. They've become broken down, almost demolished, through the course of human events. Self-led pioneers have risen from this rubble, and set out from the backdrop of broken marriages, misshapen families, and shredded communities. They've hit the wild with independence, fiercely embracing the *repulsive power of selfishness.* They've built monuments of idolatry, rather than cultures of co-laborers. They've lacked the stabilizing constitution of the Word of God to lay as cornerstone, that they might build upon the Rock. Lacking foundation, they fail to demonstrate the fullness of Kingdom of God on earth. This creates the condition of which the late Dr. Don Lynch would remark, *"We've lost kingdom culture, and we don't even know we've lost it."*

The reformation of Kingdom culture must begin with the *foundation of firsts* - the original blueprints must be reviewed that the structural supports may be rebuilt, repaired, or put back into position. The Repairer of the Breach leads the work, and incorporates pioneers who have been restored to the *foundation of firsts* as *culture reformers*. These have merged their desire for expansion to the constitutional concepts found within the King's decree. They have surrendered selfish ambition in exchange for the noble cause of ambassadorial pursuits that their diplomatic charge requires.

The King's domain reflects the King's nature, character and authority. The Kingdom expands in ever-widening circumference, bringing wholesome development to the citizens therein. The covenant of marriage, the origin point of family, is the vehicle of expansion for the Kingdom, as family lineage moves generationally through the centuries. This is not to neglect the personal responsibility of becoming born-again. Like a honeycomb, the structural support for honoring God is greatest within the cellular framework of a people who revere His ways. The natural reality of family reflects the spiritual reality of the family of God.

The Era of Reformation will produce transformation within the society of Kingdom citizens moving as one. The culture of the King will be demonstrated among all the families in the earth who are called by His Name.

This book is a beginning to that end. It is an identifying work, each chapter pointing the reader to the pieces and parts that belong as structure to the culture of the Kingdom. Honor is first given to the Builder, the Architect, as the pillars of creation are explored. Afterward, the words of Jesus frame the seven pillars of Kingdom culture as revealed in Matthew 19.

May we all *"advance from private to public affections; from the love of parents, brothers and sisters, to those more expanded regards which embrace the immense society of human kind."*

May we all discover the empowering strength that is received from the structural pillars of Kingdom culture.

In Him ~
Angela Broussard
June 2022

PART I

THE ARCHITECT OF OIKOS

& THE BLUEPRINTS OF HIS KINGDOM

Meet the Creator King, intent on building an estate of structured purpose. Generational expansion on His agenda, He chose to partner with His Heir. Sons of the Kingdom, maturing in capacity to inherit, do as the King does.

1

THE INVISIBLE KINGDOM

Jesus answered, "My kingdom is not of this world. If My kingdom were of this world, My servants would fight, so that I should not be delivered to the Jews; but now My kingdom is not from here."

— JOHN 18:36 NKJV

The arrival of the Word made flesh introduced a cataclysmic shift on earth for the kingdom of darkness. Powers and principalities, the fallen angelic beings of the resistance, hidden in abysmal structures, faced the first real threat to their encampment. The strongholds they'd built were in place to enforce their dominion, a veritable network of patterned defilement of the seed, the land, and the livelihood[1] of humanity. The illegitimate authority of the satan faced a showdown not of swords and force, but of legitimacy and judicial empowerment.

The Christ would displace the despot, through surrendering His life to the purpose of the Creator, allowing His innocent blood to soak the earth. The eternal effect of this powerful action, an action of covenant, would strip the enemy of his capacity to enforce his diabolical rule. The treasonous action of the first Adam, relinquishing the dominion of the earth, had empowered the administration of a dark, nefarious kingdom built upon the attributes of pride and jealousy.[2] Ever the deceiver, the satan held no intention of allowing the sons of men to understand his tremendous loss. Instead, he continued under the cloak of darkness, roaming the earth, seeking those whom he could devour.[3]

As Jesus walked the earth, demonstrating the dominion of the invisible Kingdom of His Father, as the second Adam, He also healed the land. Like Abraham and Joshua of old, having taken every piece of ground where their foot trod–so also did He, restoring ages of ravaging produced by the ill behavior of mankind. In His final days, He communed with Father, praying:

> *Now I am no longer in the world, but these are in the world, and I come to You. Holy Father, keep through Your name those whom You have given Me, that they may be one as We are. I have given them Your word; the world has hated them because they are not of the world, just as I am not of the world. I do not pray that You should take them out of the world, but that You should keep them from the evil one. They are not of the world, just as I am not of the world. Sanctify them by Your truth. Your word is truth. As You sent Me into the world, I also have sent them into the world. And for their sake I sanctify Myself, that they also may be sanctified by the truth.*

— JOHN 17:11; 14-16 NKJV

In a three-hour window, every joining clasp, grip, and entanglement of dark iniquity penetrated His being, as He, suffering a cross death,[4] bore the weight of humanity's previous failure. The blood price He paid ransomed humanity from the heinous oversight of the fallen host. In a moment, a twinkling, His resurrection came, and triumphantly overturned the shadow government. He delivered humanity from the power of darkness[5] and obtained the right to inherit the Kingdom from His Father, the King. Crowned the Prince of Peace,[6] Jesus conveyed us who believe into the kingdom as joint-heirs. Now, our citizenship is in heaven,[7] even as we remain in the earth. Here, we steward under His tutelage, and eagerly wait for His return.

2

THE CREATOR-KING

> *By faith we understand that the world was created by the word of God, so that what is seen was made out of things which do not appear.*

— HEBREWS 11:3 NASB

Who is this King? What is this invisible Kingdom? Does it have a discernible framework?

The Creator, the Self-Existing One, is a Spirit-Being, engaged in a creative process utilizing sound to produce the invisible and visible world.

According to the Genesis account of the beginning of creation, the heavens were first to be called a Kingdom, as an invisible sphere, or realm. As Architect of the first, the Creator determined to create a second realm, a visible sphere.

The action of creating produced ownership, and initiated His rule as King. The Greek word for king is *basileus*, meaning *governor*, or *lord over land*. Likewise, it can be rendered *a prince; a commander; a leader of the people*.

The Creator, who is the King, desired to share His governing capacity.[1] His architectural plan produced blueprints, resulting in humanity being formed and fashioned from the clay of the earth, and made after His image. The first son, Adam, was given a guardian-protector task of all the Creator-King owned. Humanity, in Adam, carried His likeness, His spirit nature, as a son.

Endowed with the *onoma*, the nature, character, and authority[2] of God, obedience was required of Adam. The requirement centered around a governmental function, that of jurisdiction, represented by two trees: the tree of life, and the tree of the knowledge of good and evil. Should the created son honor the instruction of the Creator-King, not to eat of the tree of knowledge, the created son would mature to the position of inheritor of all. Faltering between the directive concerning the two trees, the first son quickly discovered the consequence of treason. He failed to legislate according to the decree he had been given: he surrendered the capacity to govern. Adam relinquished jurisdictional powers to a faithless foe.

When Jesus arose as the second Adam, a son willing to obey the directives of dominion, He demonstrated how the invisible Kingdom is to rule, dominate and influence the seen realm. The *basilea*, the land owned by the *basileus*, or Creator-King, was regarded as Royal Domain.

The terms *basileus* and *basilea* are derived from the Greek word *basis*. *Basis* describes the function of *walking, stepping, placing one's foot upon*. The territory which the King walks upon is that which is governed by the King.

Therefore, Jesus matured His sonship by obedience, submitting to the decrees originally given to the first son, Adam: first, He was to walk the land, harnessing it again to the Creator-King, the Architect, through dominion. Second, He was to walk in the spirit-nature, the *onoma*, of the Creator-King. Third, He spoke, issuing the sound of the King's decrees. Jesus, through loyal obedience, matured His sonship to the position of inheritor, and has inherited the Kingdom of His Father.

The Creator-King created with sound, revealed Himself by sound, and demonstrated His likeness in the earth as sound, the Word, made flesh. As the inhabitants of the earth beheld the glory of Eyeh Asher Eyeh[3]–or I AM–they beheld Spirit, for I AM is Spirit. The spiritual force of the Word in human likeness, of the man Jesus, revealed that the Kingdom was of spiritual nature. His actions reveal, through intangible attributes, that true governing power is a spiritual function.

For the kingdom of God is not in word but in power.

— 1 CORINTHIANS 4:20 KJV

The kingdom of God is not eating and drinking, but right-eousness and peace and joy in the Holy Spirit.

— ROMANS 14:17 KJV

The kingdom of God does not come with observation; nor will they say, 'See here!' or 'See there!' For indeed, the kingdom of God is within you."

— LUKE 17:20-21 NKJV

3

THE CREATOR-KING AS ARCHITECT

> *By faith Abram lived as a stranger in the land of promise, as in a foreign land, living in tents with Isaac and Jacob, fellow heirs of the same promise; for he was looking for the city which has foundations,[1] whose architect and builder is God.*

— HEBREWS 11:9-10 NASB

An architect is one who plans, calculates and constructs. Beginning with abstract thought, an architect will compile a design idea, and bring it forth in descriptive terms in order to produce the image crafted by thought. Transforming an idea from an abstract condition to a produced, finished product requires language. For the builder, two types of language are used. First is that of sound–communication through words–which describe what is to be built. Second is that of drawing blueprints, also known as schematics, line drawings that transform the idea into a tangibly viewed concept.

Abram sought a city that had spiritual foundations. Were he to find that City, he would also meet a Craftsman of the highest caliber, the Architect. God, the Creator-King, built His invisible City upon eternal principles, likened unto blueprints, that support life, family, community and culture. The power and capacity of this invisible City, part of the invisible Kingdom, now impresses its attributes upon the visible realm.

In order to consider the framework of this invisible-made-visible Kingdom, we look to the father of faith. The writer of Hebrews tells us that Abraham, previously known as Abram, followed an irresistible draw by the Spirit of God, calling him to leave the ancient Mesopotamian city, Ur of Chaldees. Abram's upbringing in this city exposed him to cultural underpinnings based upon the worship of false deities. The empty practice of worshiping the moon was a manner of living that left Abram wanting. He longed for the security of something eternal, something lasting. He was seeking the Truth upon which the first principles of creation,[2] the *foundation of firsts*, were instituted–that of an unseen realm governing the seen.

Creator-King utilized Abram's longing for an enduring place of habitation, and chose to introduce Himself. Drawing Abram into a relationship, Creator-King specified a journey for him to embark. The journey was lengthy, and led him to the region of Canaan, which would one day be termed Israel. In the new land, the Creator invested deeply in a covenant of friendship[3] with Abram, imparting to the man a portion of His Name. As Abram experienced the sound-merge of Creator-King's name, *eyeh*, embedded within his own, Abraham, began to experience expansion in his trade capacity as a skilled agrarian businessman. He was soon surrounded with immense increase.

However, Abraham remained dissatisfied. He continually felt a sense of longing he could not quite describe, causing him to cast a watchful eye on the horizon for a place of habitation, a city he could not see – the city whose maker and builder was God Himself.

Abraham represents all humanity: individuals seeking a healthy experience and expression of life, family, community and culture.

In His infinite wisdom, Creator-King made provision for the invisible Kingdom attributes to produce a mirror image of itself upon the visible realm. This imaging function is the blueprint of the Kingdom. The transfer of the schematic imprint is carried upon the provision of Wisdom, the bedrock foundation upon which all structural components are built. The foundation, joints, fasteners connect the invisible to the visible through the action of Covenant.

4

BLUEPRINTS & SCHEMATICS

Then the channels of the sea were seen, The foundations of the world were uncovered At Your rebuke, O Lord, At the blast of the breath of Your nostrils.

— PSALM 18:15 NKJV

ncient text provides a poetic backdrop to the unseen structure supporting the earth. The *'blast of the breath of God,'* or, *nashamah*, rolled back the blanket of creation to reveal the hidden underpinnings, the foundations of the world. Modern architects might call such foundational pillars 'pylons,' a word describing great lengths of steel beams pounded into the earth, providing tremendous strength to hold a skyscraper upright.

The Foundational Pillars

In the Hebrew language, the word for foundation is *amud.*[1] Amud has three definitive descriptions. First, *amud* is defined as *great pillars, depicted by upright columns of smoke and fire.* As the foundations of the earth, these provided a platform to sustain the pottery of Creator King's hands. Not unlike an easel to hold artwork in a gallery, the pillars of the earth hold the finished product on display.

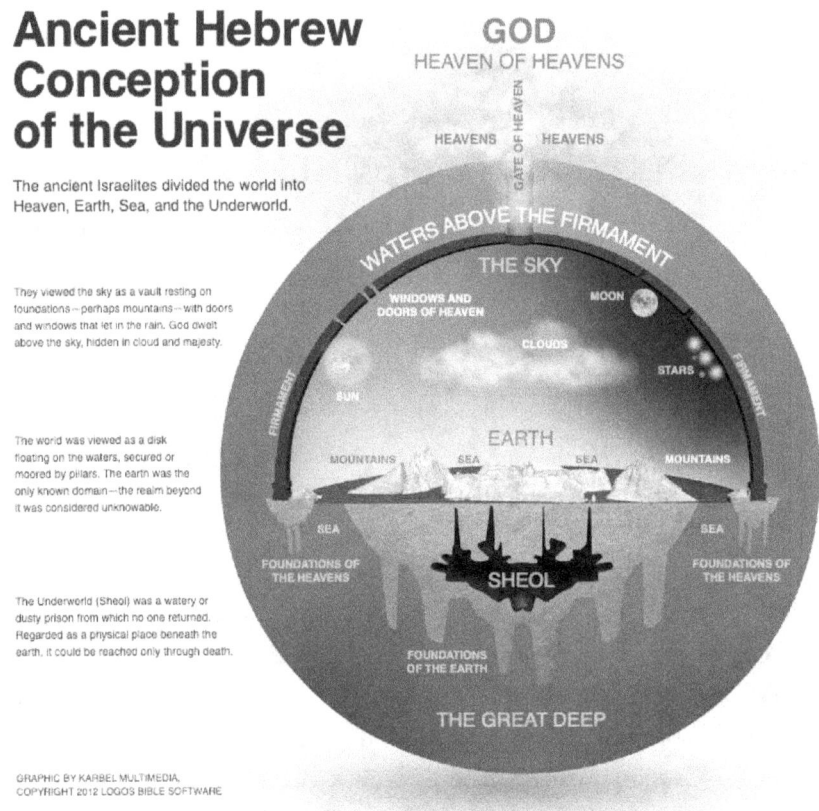

Ancient Hebrew Conception of the Universe

The ancient Israelites divided the world into Heaven, Earth, Sea, and the Underworld.

They viewed the sky as a vault resting on foundations—perhaps mountains—with doors and windows that let in the rain. God dwelt above the sky, hidden in cloud and majesty.

The world was viewed as a disk floating on the waters, secured or moored by pillars. The earth was the only known domain—the realm beyond it was considered unknowable.

The Underworld (Sheol) was a watery or dusty prison from which no one returned. Regarded as a physical place beneath the earth, it could be reached only through death.

GOD
HEAVEN OF HEAVENS
HEAVENS — GATE OF HEAVEN — HEAVENS
WATERS ABOVE THE FIRMAMENT
THE SKY
WINDOWS AND DOORS OF HEAVEN
MOON
CLOUDS
STARS
FIRMAMENT
SUN
EARTH
MOUNTAINS — SEA — SEA — MOUNTAINS
SEA
SEA
FOUNDATIONS OF THE HEAVENS
FOUNDATIONS OF THE HEAVENS
SHEOL
FOUNDATIONS OF THE EARTH
THE GREAT DEEP

GRAPHIC BY KARBEL MULTIMEDIA.
COPYRIGHT 2012 LOGOS BIBLE SOFTWARE

The hidden pilings are described in the book of Job 9:6 and 26:11, respectively: *He shakes the earth out of its place, and its pillars tremble. The pillars of heaven tremble, and are astonished at His rebuke.*

Amud can also depict scaffolding. Similar to an easel, yet utilized to scale the height of a wall or building, scaffolding allows construction to take place. Various elements can be applied to the pillars to cover them, hiding them from view with a covering pleasant to the eyes. A workman will stand on a scaffold in order to reach the vertical space, and be supported by the scaffold while he works. Because the work on a scaffold is done above ground, additional support pillars are secured to the pillars that have been positioned beneath the ground. Together, the pillars above and the pillars beneath give substance to hold the finished work together.

Finally, the third definition of *amud* presents as a verb meaning: *to take a stand; to cause to set up as erect; endure.* It is used in this context in 2 Kings 23:3.

> *Then the king [Josiah] stood by a pillar [amud] and made a covenant before the Lord, to follow the Lord and to keep His commandments and His testimonies and His statutes, with all his heart and all his soul, to perform the words of this covenant that were written in this book. And all the people took a stand for the covenant.*

— 2 KINGS 23:3 NKJV

Josiah's position next to the pillar became a visible representation of *how* the Covenant of the Lord provided a framework for life, creating stability and blessing - a scaffold of support. Standing beside the pillar was a visual demonstration of *the action of his commitment* to the Covenant, as he publicly announced he was going to act on the directives of the Pentateuch.[2] His declarative action compelled his constituents to do likewise. The Covenant literally gave the nation the ability to set their jaw, as it were; to stand erect and endure.

Josiah agreed with the scroll of Word he found. The Covenant word became both the foundation and the pillar of his position.

The same holds true for those who honor the Word of God as the bedrock of life. The Word becomes the foundation and causes one to stand upright in enduring integrity.

The Structural Pillars

> *Wisdom has built her house; she has hewn out her seven pillars.*

— PROVERBS 9:1 NASB

The foundation of a building requires a strong platform, be it pylons or a firm bed. Likewise, the upright, visible portion of the building must also contain support: pillars beneath and pillars above. Yet, a structure without the essence of life within is simply a building. A home requires inhabitants, namely individuals who bring vim and vigor, love and laughter, delight and direction. Mental and emotional stimuli must be produced through the exchange of language to provide context for family.

At first glance, it appears that Wisdom is only concerned with structure - a calculated construction void of the essence of life. Yet Wisdom herself is infused with life. What is Wisdom's intention in building these seven pillars?

In *sod*[3] fashion, a deeper look reveals that Wisdom is not merely building an edifice ... **The house that Wisdom is building is a son!** The hidden element of this exciting revelation is found in the Hebraic word for 'built' in Proverbs 9:1. *Built* in the passage above is *banah*, or, *ben*, meaning: son. The term *ben* is not passive, rather, it denotes a son as *a builder of a family name*, or, in the widest sense, *the name of a household*. Creator-King's image-bearers, His sons, are being built into a spiritual house!

To understand this concept fully, consider the most fundamental structure in the universe: that of a household. The Hebraic word for father is *ab*, from which the term *abba* is derived. Biblically, the role of a father is to raise up sons who regard Creator-King. The role of a son is to continue the vision and governance of the father over his house. Creator-King chose Abraham for his capacity to do this very thing:

For I have chosen him, so that he may command his children and his household after him to keep the way of the LORD by doing righteousness and justice.

— GENESIS 18:19 NKJV

Proverbs 30:1 presents the concept of generational continuation to the purpose of building a house - a household - that honors Creator-King. In coy fashion, the wisdom literature tucks away, hidden from direct view, a gem discovered through the use of names. Utilizing the meaning behind the spoken name, the names themselves create a sentence. The sentence uncovered describes the action of an *abba*, as he raises up sons to inherit his vision, learn his trade, and continue the family name, all while maintaining respect toward Creator-King. The verse begins: *The words of Agur the son of Jakeh, the pronouncement. The man declares to Ithiel, to Ithiel and Ucal ...*

Modern translations render Agur as *the son of* Jakeh, however, in the original text, it reads, Agur *ben* Jakeh - a son, notably carrying on the purpose for which he has been brought forth: to build the family name. How are these names defined? Agur means *collector*, or *gatherer, to gather wages*. Ithiel defined means *God is with me*. Ucal is defined as *I am strong, I will prevail*. Thus, as a collective saying, the names can be rendered: "*Gather a harvest* [agur] *of sons* [ben] *who are blameless* [jakeh] *and obedient. They will have God with them* [itheil], *and they will be strong and mighty* [ucal]."

The Hebraic concept of the building of a house includes dynasties, expanding beyond individual family units. Since sons, *ben*, are to build the family name of the house of their fathers, one can view the panorama of Scripture and see the expansion of the chosen people into a mighty nation - a house, for Creator-King. Abraham is the most prolific of the old Covenant, and the starting point for the development of a dynasty: a multitude of generations that are so numerous they are as the sands of the sea. King David's son, Solomon, openly requested the *chockmah*, or wisdom of God in order to build the physical house of the Lord. However, the preeminent inheritor, able to build the house of Creator-King, is Jesus.

> *Christ was faithful as a Son over His house—whose house we are, if we hold firmly to our confidence and the boast of our hope.*

> — HEBREWS 3:6 BSB

Wisdom is encapsulated and personified in Jesus. Jesus, as a Son, becomes the wisdom of God, to them that believe.

> *... Of Him you are in Christ Jesus, who became for us wisdom from God—and righteousness and sanctification and redemption—*

> — 1 CORINTHIANS 1:30 NKJV

Through His preeminence, sonship is made available to any who will enter the same covenant relationship of friendship Creator-King made with Abraham. Jesus, through His obedience and sacrifice, became the first-fruits example of one who is able to gather a harvest of sons who are blameless and obedient.

Jesus rose as Son, fully accepted and authorized to inherit what Creator-King had made. His inheritance is shared among those who believe. **We are part of a living structure of sonship, a house, an *oikos*, intended before the foundation of the world.**

> *Moses indeed was faithful in all His house as a servant, for a testimony of those things which would be spoken afterward, but Christ as a Son over His own house, <u>whose house we are</u> if we hold fast the confidence and the rejoicing of the hope firm to the end.*

> — HEBREWS 3:5-6 NKJV

Peter the apostle reiterates the truth that we are living stones, set into the structure of a building, a house:

> *... coming to Him as to a living stone which has been rejected by people, but is choice and precious in the sight of God, you also, as living stones, are being built up as a spiritual house for a holy priesthood, to offer spiritual sacrifices that are acceptable to God through Jesus Christ.*

— 1 PETER 2:4-5 NASB

> *This house is built upon a solid, firm foundation: I also say to you that you are Peter, and on this rock I will build My church, and the gates of Hades shall not prevail against it.*

— MATTHEW 16:18 BSB

> *Therefore whoever hears these sayings of Mine, and does them, I will liken him to a wise man who built his house on the rock: and the rain descended, the floods came, and the winds blew and beat on that house; and it did not fall, for it was founded on the rock. "But everyone who hears these sayings of Mine, and does not do them, will be like a foolish man who built his house on the sand: and the rain descended, the floods came, and the winds blew and beat on that house; and it fell. And great was its fall."*

— MATTHEW 7:24-27 NKJV

As Abraham of old, we regard Creator-King as Architect and Builder of this house, recognizing the spiritual substance of which it is made.

ANGELA BROUSSARD

 Unless the Lord builds the house, They labor in vain who build it.

— PSALM 127:1 NASB

5

ATTRIBUTES OF KINGDOM

 The Lord is our judge; The Lord is our lawgiver; The Lord is our king—He will save us!

— ISAIAH 33:22 NASB

Having identified the Creator-King, and the origination of His architectural layout for His Kingdom, it is now possible to consider the practical ramifications of the foundations developed thus far. There are certain characteristics common to all kingdoms.

The facets of a kingdom begin with a king. A king rules over a territory and has a community of subjects. The subjects carry privileges as citizens, and are afforded an acceptable lifestyle governed by a code of ethical conduct within the kingdom called a commonwealth. The system of societal norms within that commonwealth carries protocol and procedures, as well as an embedded economic security. All of this is governed by a royal covenant, or constitution, with legal and accepted principles within established boundaries. The borders of the kingdom are then protected by an army.

The Kingdom of God, according to Jesus, possesses these components, or attributes, even though invisible to the naked eye. To understand the integral parts of the invisible Kingdom,[1] a closer look at a natural kingdom will aid understanding.

What is a Kingdom

A kingdom cannot exist without a king. *The King*, a sovereign, is considered supreme or preeminent in a particular group or sphere. As sovereign, authority flows from the king, placing his word as notable above all others.

The Territory, or, Domain is the region over which the king exercises total authority. Inside the boundaries of this land, the sovereign king has jurisdictional power. The complete ownership of the king includes all resources: land, minerals, water, as well as persons, each the property of the king.

> *The Earth is the Lord's and the fullness thereof; the world, and they that dwell therein ...*

— PSALMS 24:1 KJV

The Constitution is the covenant, or agreement, which the king utilizes as a means to express his desire to care for and partner with the citizens of his kingdom. The constitution documents the words of the king, describing his intent. Within this written treatise are the benefits and privileges provided in his kingdom. The Bible contains the constitution of the Kingdom of God which details His will that He has in mind for His citizens.

The Citizenry describes the collective of people that live under the rule of the king. The king takes up his covenant provision in order to care for and protect those who have entered his kingdom. The welfare of the citizens is always a king's strong consideration, as the care of his constituents is a reflection upon himself. The citizenry, receiving the covenant provision, choose to yield to the king in order to be in right standing with him.

Citizenship in the invisible Kingdom of God is obtained by becoming born again, at which point an individual is able to access the spiritual understanding of the Kingdom.

 Jesus responded and said to him, "Truly, truly, I say to you, unless someone is born again he cannot see the kingdom of God.

— JOHN 3:3 NASB

In the Kingdom of God, yielding to the King is called righteousness, and furthers the relationship between the King and his citizens. The relationship between the King and His people is a priority of both parties, which is why Jesus instructed: *But seek first his kingdom and his righteousness, and all these things will be given to you as well* (Matthew 6:33).

The Law is an extension of the constitution, establishing the standards and principles by which the kingdom will be administered. These are set by the king himself. The laws convey standards of conduct, and are designed to be obeyed by all, including visitors and foreigners. To violate the laws of the kingdom places one at odds with the king. The laws in a kingdom cannot be changed by the citizens, nor are they subject to a citizen referendum or debate. Simply put, the word of the king is law in his kingdom. Rebellion against the law is rebellion against the king. King David understood this principle of the royal word when he stated, *I will bow down toward your Holy Temple and will praise your name for your love and your faithfulness, for you have exalted above all things your name and your word* (Psalm 138: 2-3).

A Code of Ethics defines the acceptable conduct of citizens in the kingdom. The adherence to a code of moral standards, social relationships, and manner of life affects their representation of the kingdom. Closely related to the constitution and law, yet allowing for nuance of region and expression, this code includes moral standards, social relationships, personal conduct, attitude, attire, and manner of life.

The Army of a kingdom functions to secure the domain of the king. This includes property, resources, and citizens. Kingdom citizens enjoy the protection of the army, while some constituents also participate in the military strategy of the army.

In the Kingdom of God, the army is identified as the angelic host of heaven. The angelic host responds to the word of the King, including the word of the King spoken and reiterated by the citizenry. In this way, the declaration of the word of the King releases the angelic host to their assignment, namely to secure the boundaries of the Kingdom.

> *He unleashed against them His hot anger, His wrath, indignation and hostility a band of destroying angels.*

— PSALM 78:49 NASB

> *Praise the Lord, you His angels, you mighty ones who do His bidding, who obey His word. Praise the Lord all His heavenly host, you His servants who do His will.*

— PSALM 103:20-21 NIV

> *So it will be at the end of the age. The Son of Man will send out His angels, and they will weed out of His kingdom everything that causes sin and all who do evil. They will throw them into the fiery furnace, where there will be weeping and gnashing of teeth.*

— MATTHEW 13:40B-42 BSB

A Commonwealth[2] when spoken of in Scripture reflects the Greek word politeia. Politeia defines the condition of a citizen, or, the relation in which a citizen stands with the state. In a kingdom, the term *commonwealth* is used because the king's desire is that all his citizens share and benefit from the wealth of the kingdom.

Jesus expresses the will of the King for His citizens by saying:

> *... I tell you, do not worry about your life, what you will eat; or about your body, what you will wear. Life is more than food, and the body more than clothes.*

— LUKE 12:22-23 BSB

> *But seek His kingdom, and these things will be given to you as well. Do not be afraid, little flock, for your Father has been pleased to give you the kingdom.*

— LUKE 12:31-32 NIV

As all of these attributes of a kingdom are brought together, it becomes clear that the attributes create a structure for the **Social Culture** of its people. Social Culture is the environment created by the life and manners of the king and his citizens. As this unique ecosystem of behavior is given expression corporately, it is distinguished from among all other cultures in comparison. The Kingdom of God expresses the nature, character, and authority of its King. Kingdom social culture is to be evident in our daily activities and encounters.

Of Kings and Priests

> *Neither shall they say, Lo here! or, lo there! for, behold, the kingdom of God is within you.*

— LUKE 17:21 KJV

Having identified the king, as well as the attributes and components of a kingdom, a framework has been portrayed. It is now possible to introduce a powerful truth, a most unique feature of the Kingdom of God. In this feature, the King's desire to share his governing capacity is seen: the citizens of the King are kings themselves.

> *Jesus Christ, the faithful witness, the firstborn from the dead, and the ruler over the kings of the earth ...to Him who loved us and washed us from our sins in His own blood, **has made us kings and priests to His God and Father,** to Him be glory and dominion forever and ever. Amen.*

— REVELATION 1:6 NKJV

> *Until the Ancient of days came, and judgment was given to the saints of the most High; and the time came that the saints possessed the kingdom.*

— DANIEL 7:22 KJV

> *... the kingdom and dominion, and the greatness of the kingdom under the whole heaven, shall be given to the people of the saints of the most High ...*

— DANIEL 7:27 KJV

Kingship resides in every believer, positionally. Growth and maturity in sonship provides the path toward ruling and reigning as a joint-heir of Christ, a king, experientially. The practical aspects of kingdom development are now able to be added to the framework. The additional pieces will be found in the constitutional make-up of the Kingdom of God, which will be discussed next.

6

CONSTITUTIONAL STABILITY

The kingdom is the Lord's: and He is the governor among the nations.

— PSALM 22:28 KJV

The Creator-King caused His invisible Kingdom to be known and understood by the first Adam. The spoken word describing His Kingdom traveled generations through Enoch, Noah, Abraham, and ultimately extended to a nation of people. Abraham's leadership success as an *abba* is proven in the demonstration of the Tribes of Israel. Each maintained an identity as a family unit, even when enslaved by Egypt. The corporate body of tribes grew in number over a four hundred year period, even as Moses rose as leader.

Moses was a Hebrew by birth. He was of the household of Levi, yet due to the oppression of the nation as a whole, his mother stowed him away in a basket on the river Nile. Soon discovered by an Egyptian princess, Moses was brought into the house of Pharoah, and raised as his son, an Egyptian royal. Trained in governmental protocol and procedure, he had been raised to inherit Egypt.

Proximity to the opulence of Pharaoh's household made him well-versed in divination practices. The Egyptians worshiped Hwt-Ptah,[1] a counterfeit creator-god, among others, and even revered Pharoah as a deity. Yet, for all the benefit offered him as an up and coming regent, Moses came in contact with his own people daily, while they served the country that had given their forefathers refuge in the Great Famine. From this vantage point, Moses could recognize that the covenant agreement between Abraham and Creator-King had been held in high regard among the tribes. They worshiped in a unified expression of familiarity with their God, as though Creator-King were intimately involved in their daily lives. The demonstration of honor toward Abraham's God had become their own, having been maintained generationally through the telling and retelling of the ways in which God had revealed His nature by keeping His word. The stories told of how Joseph had been sold into slavery to the greatest nation on the earth, and became second only to Pharoah in the land of Egypt reverberated among the people as they worked. Even though now in servitude, they were a stable people.

The knowledge of Creator-King was alive and well.

His Name had been preserved.

Moses witnessed the rough behavior of the ruling class, the royal regime, toward the people with whom he shared a bloodline. The flicker of purpose rose within him, as he supposed his native people recognized he was to be, like Joseph, their deliverer. Moses was stunned to discover his native people did not hold the same vision, as he moved against an Egyptian,[2] in order to repair an injustice. Witnesses to the murder he'd committed created a murmuring among the Hebrew nation. Once discovered, and now afraid for his life, Moses abruptly departed from his leadership position among the Egyptian elite.

For forty years, Moses hid in the desert, pleased to have spared his own life. Here, he shed the formality of the ways of the Egyptian government. He also turned away from the customs of covenant with the God of the Hebrew people. The obscurity allowed him a form of freedom, but, as Abraham of old, Moses could not shake a sense of longing that gave him pause to enter into true contentment.

Ultimately, his true calling would be awoken by a spark, a fire, in the midst of a bush that would not burn.[3] Initiated by curiosity, Moses found himself face-to-face in a transformational encounter with the true Creator-King. Here, he received his assignment: he was called to confront the counterfeit creator Hwt-Ptah, and the cabal of Egyptian deities worshiped at the royal palace of Pharaoh.

In order to fulfill the assignment, Moses had to return to the worldly house that had spared his life. His loyalty to the house of the false creator, Hwt-Ptah, would be overturned, and he would rise as leader among the Hebrews in earnest. The Hebrew nation, molded by four hundred years of servitude, was about to encounter Moses, the deliverer. He would convey the attributes and identifiers of the invisible Kingdom to those fresh from captivity. Creator-King would partner with Moses as His representative, through the spoken and written word.

The language of the Covenant was to find itself in documented form. The Word of Creator-King would become a constitution, a law, a set of governing boundaries. The boundaries would depict the moral standards, social relationships, personal conduct, attitude, attire, and manner of life of the Hebrew nation.

The multitude would benefit from the blueprints of creation, freshly articulated. These blueprints were instructions. The instructions Moses received came to be known as the Torah. Torah is both a name and a concept, derived from two words, *tor* and *yara*. Both have a verb and noun meaning. The noun form of Torah is at the *pashat*[4] level of understanding; the verb is at the *remez*.[5]

Torah:		
Tor	*noun*	Dove
Yara	*noun*	Refers to rain and/or teacher; a set of instructions
Torah:		
Tor	*verb*	To explore or survey, in broad circular or sweeping motion
Yara	*verb*	To bring about by a unifying effect by means of many little impulses

The verb roots reveal that the progression of instruction brings about a united effect by many little impulses in succession. By studying these two layers together, the Torah, then, reveals there is an archetype of process through which everything moves, grows and matures. It doesn't simply state how things should be– rather, the word Torah reflects how things are. Through the Torah, the very creation is a blueprint, where all the *firsts* and *'in the beginnings,'* reveal how Creator-King intended to move, maintaining dominion and ownership of His creation.

Translation To The New

Distilled as a law or teaching, the religious leaders of Jesus' day established the Torah as an overbearing rule and regulation. Boundaries and best practices are included in constitutional writ. Rules and regulations can provide training and bring about healthy relationships according to Romans 7:7: *I would not have known sin were it not for the law.* However, the religious leaders were reducing the Torah to a thought process, a figment of their own imagination. The premise put forth by these teachers of the law was based upon a worldly view of the words on the scroll. Focused on the minutiae of the letter, and the development of additional clauses, the rabbinical leadership ultimately developed a rigid legal structure, superimposing their code upon the Creator-King's blueprints and seeking to rule their own view of kingdom over the greater population.

When Jesus came as Rabbi, He upended their thought processes.

He properly placed Covenant before formal law. He understood the words of the Torah were spirit in nature, capable of producing faith. The Torah was not to be reduced to the letter, it was to be a reflection of the natural law, such as the writer of Romans 2:14 described:

> *..when Gentiles, who do not have the law, by nature do the things in the law, these, although not having the law, are a law to themselves, who show the work of the law written in their hearts, their conscience also bearing witness, and between themselves their thoughts accusing or else excusing them.*[6]

Speaking as Teacher, Jesus' origination point was from the place of 'how things are.' His origination point was truth, because He was, and is, Truth–the Word made flesh.

> *All the people were speaking well of Him, and admiring the gracious words which were coming from His lips; and yet they were saying, "Is this not Joseph's son?"*
>
> — LUKE 4:22 NASB

Jesus was speaking from the blueprint He received directly from Creator-King, and He didn't veer from it. He followed what was written in assignment and in alignment with the Architect. As a result, Authority backed His words. After all, they were His blueprints to begin with.

> *I will open My mouth in parables; I will utter things hidden since the foundation of the world.*
>
> — MATTHEW 13:35 BSB

The Torah was a spiritual treatise that Jesus embodied, taken upon Himself in fullness as the Holy Spirit in the form of a dove [*tor*] descended [*yara*] upon Him. Jesus, who has been made unto us wisdom, righteousness, sanctification, walked according to the fullness of the Word in His era, so that He could fulfill the prophecies; every jot and tittle of the law.

> *For verily I say unto you, Till heaven and earth pass, one jot or one tittle shall in no wise pass from the law, till all be fulfilled.*

> — MATTHEW 5:18 NKJV

His obedience to the Torah provided a new and living way, producing a new covenant–a new constitution, as it were–founded upon better principles than the blood of bulls and goats.

Stability is Vital for Growth.

The Torah, as a document of natural expression, creates a form of societal norms, customs or manners a populace will use to determine their lifestyle. To the religious mindset, these are rules and regulations. A religious environment will elevate the letter of the law above the spiritual substance of the Word. However, the Word, which is Spirit, brings right relationship, first with Creator-King, then the seed, the land, and the livelihood.

> *...who also made us adequate as servants of a new covenant, not of the letter but of the Spirit; for the letter kills, but the Spirit gives life.*

> — 2 CORINTHIANS 3:6 NASB

Throughout the process of spirit-first instruction, the Torah, the Word made flesh, produces stability.

Stability is a prerequisite for all growth and maturation.

Stability is required to bring about progress.

We become born again by the incorruptible seed of the Word of God. The Word germinates the process of bringing about a unified effect of sanctification and renewal–by means of many little impulses–causing maturation. What does maturity look like? It is the harvest of the Word made flesh in us, driven by an obedience to the spiritual constitution, the Covenant, culminating in love. Love is the fulfillment of the Torah.

> *Owe nothing to anyone except to love one another; for the one who loves his neighbor has fulfilled the Law. For this, "You shall not commit adultery, You shall not murder, You shall not steal, You shall not covet," and if there is any other commandment, it is summed up in this saying, "You shall love your neighbor as yourself." Love does no wrong to a neighbor; therefore love is the fulfillment of the Law.*

— ROMANS 13:8-10 NASB

> *And He said to him, "'You shall love the Lord your God with all your heart, and with all your soul, and with all your mind.' This is the great and foremost commandment. The second is like it, 'You shall love your neighbor as yourself.'*

— MATTHEW 22:37-39 NASB

As Jesus was crowned Prince of Peace,[7] or *shalom [shalem]*, He embodied the effect of *shalom* among all Kingdom citizens. The word means more than peace. It represents wholeness, wellness, well-being, safety, happiness, friendliness, favor, completeness, security, prosperity, and to be victorious. The pictographic symbols for the word *shalom* (*shin, lamad, vav, mem*) read, *"Destroy the authority that binds to chaos."* As a noun, shalom is derived from the verb form *shalam*, which means "to restore" in a sense of replacing or providing what is needed to make someone or something whole and complete. *Shalom* crushes chaos.

Without question, the Kingdom of God brings stability to chaotic environments.

Exercising the constitution of the Word, this new covenant produces change and atmospheric shift. Each precept added produces greater and deeper stability within. The Word is the stability of our times. That's the Torah, that's the blueprint, the Word of God. Now written on the table of the human heart.

> *Bind them upon thy fingers, write them upon the table of thine heart.*

— PROVERBS 7:3 KJV

> *... the words that I have spoken to you are spirit, and are life.*

— JOHN 6:63 NASB

7

WISDOM DEPLOYS THE BLUEPRINT

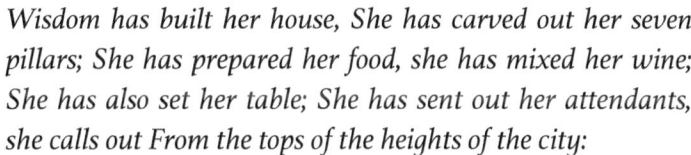

Wisdom has built her house, She has carved out her seven pillars; She has prepared her food, she has mixed her wine; She has also set her table; She has sent out her attendants, she calls out From the tops of the heights of the city:

"Whoever is naive, let him turn in here!"
   To him who lacks understanding she says,
   "Come, eat of my food
   And drink of the wine I have mixed.
   Abandon your foolishness and live,
   And proceed in the way of understanding."

— PROVERBS 9:1-6 NASB

A fter a query of Kingdom rank had emerged from His disciples, Jesus posits a dialogue on the invisible kingdom. Matthew's account of the conversation shares His discourse, and makes way for instruction of *the way things are,* reflected inside the culture among the citizenry of God's Kingdom. Jesus effectively translates the letter of the Torah into the Spirit-first substance of Wisdom personified in the realm of the New Covenant. In so doing, wisdom establishes an environment: *a culture* - that allows the predominant expressions of the nature, character, and authority of the Creator-King to be released. Impacting behavior and attitude of social groups and organizations, this culture is founded upon the governmental precepts of the Word through Wisdom's revelatory action. This work defines the cultural discussion, parsed to seven topics, or pillars.

The seven pillars of Wisdom have been recognized in various ways: the seven spirits of God, the seven days of creation, even the seven attributes of wisdom spoken of by the Apostle James. In the following section, from the springboard of Matthew 19, Wisdom's pillars, will be considered visible, actionable, structural pillars of the invisible, living kingdom: the Kingdom of God. The invisible kingdom is recognized as an *oikos*, purposed to develop sons, constructed to reflect the King and His ways, from before the foundation of the world.

The fear of the Lord is the beginning of wisdom, And the knowledge of the Holy One is understanding. For by me your days will be multiplied, And years of life will be added to you. If you are wise, you are wise for yourself, And if you scoff, you alone will suffer from it.

— PROVERBS 9:10-12 NASB

PART II

THE ARCHITECT OF OIKOS

& THE PILLARS OF KINGDOM CULTURE

When the perfecting of kingdom principles occurs throughout a region, a new culture develops, bringing God's perfect order. We call this culture the Kingdom of God, and it's occupants the ekklesia. This culture of distinction represents a kingdom of identity synonymous with God's purpose.

— REBECCA D BENNETT, THE DESTINY SERIES
PURPOSE

KINGDOM CULTURE BLUEPRINT

FOR A SOUND HOUSE

Matthew 19

Pillar One: Oneness In Marriage

When Jesus had finished these words, He left Galilee and came into the region of Judea beyond the Jordan; and large crowds followed Him, and He healed them there.

Some Pharisees came to Jesus, testing Him and asking, "Is it lawful for a man to divorce his wife for any reason at all?" And He answered and said, "Have you not read that He who created them from the beginning made them male and female, and said, 'For this reason a man shall leave his father and his mother and be joined to his wife, and the two shall become one flesh'? So they are no longer two, but one flesh. Therefore, what God has joined together, no person is to separate." They *said to Him, "Why, then, did Moses command to give her a certificate of divorce and send her away?" He *said to them, "Because of your hardness of heart Moses permitted you to divorce your wives; but from the beginning it has not been this way. And I say to you, whoever divorces his wife, except for sexual immorality, and marries another woman commits adultery."

The disciples said to Him, "If the relationship of the man with his wife is like this, it is better not to marry." But He said to them, "Not all men can accept this statement, but only those to whom it has been given. For there are eunuchs who were born that way from their mother's womb; and there are eunuchs who were made eunuchs by people; and there are also eunuchs who made themselves eunuchs for the sake of the kingdom of heaven. The one who is able to accept this, let him accept it."

Pillar Two: The Expansion of Family

Then some children were brought to Him so that He would lay His hands on them and pray; and the disciples rebuked them. But Jesus said, "Leave the children alone, and do not forbid them to come to Me; for the kingdom of heaven belongs to such as these." After laying His hands on them, He departed from there.

Pillar Three: Sons in Relationship

And someone came to Him and said, "Teacher, what good thing shall I do so that I may obtain eternal life?" And He said to him, "Why are you asking Me about what is good? There is only One who is good; but if you want to enter life, keep the commandments." Then he *said to Him, "Which ones?" And Jesus said, "You shall not commit murder; You shall not commit adultery; You shall not steal; You shall not give false testimony; Honor your father and mother; and You shall love your neighbor as yourself." The young man *said to Him, "All these I have kept; what am I still lacking?"

Pillar Four: Occupation: Stewardship

Jesus said to him, "If you want to be complete, go and sell your possessions and give to the poor, and you will have treasure in heaven; and come, follow Me." But when the young man heard this statement, he went away grieving; for he was one who owned much property.

And Jesus said to His disciples, "Truly I say to you, it will be hard for a rich person to enter the kingdom of heaven. And again I say to you, it is easier for a camel to go through the eye of a needle, than for a rich person to enter the kingdom of God." When the disciples heard this, they were very astonished and said, "Then who can be saved?" And looking at them, Jesus said to them, "With people this is impossible, but with God all things are possible."

Pillar Five: Kingdom Economy & Commerce

Then Peter responded and said to Him, "Behold, we have left everything and followed You; what then will there be for us?"

Pillar Six: Kingdom Authority

And Jesus said to them, "Truly I say to you, that you who have followed Me, in the regeneration when the Son of Man will sit on His glorious throne, you also shall sit upon twelve thrones, judging the twelve tribes of Israel. And everyone who has left houses or brothers or sisters or father or mother or children or farms on account of My name, will receive many times as much, and will inherit eternal life.

Pillar Seven: Worship The King

But many who are first will be last; and the last, first.

8

COVENANT ONENESS IN MARRIAGE

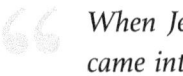

When Jesus had finished these words, He left Galilee and came into the region of Judea beyond the Jordan; and large crowds followed Him, and He healed them there.

Some Pharisees came to Jesus, testing Him and asking, "Is it lawful for a man to divorce his wife for any reason at all?" And He answered and said, "Have you not read that He who created them from the beginning made them male and female, and said, 'For this reason a man shall leave his father and his mother and be joined to his wife, and the two shall become one flesh'? So they are no longer two, but one flesh. Therefore, what God has joined together, no person is to separate." They said to Him, "Why, then, did Moses command to give her a certificate of divorce and send her away?" He *said to them, "Because of your hardness of heart Moses permitted you to divorce your wives; but from the beginning it has not been this way. And I say to you, whoever divorces his wife, except for sexual immorality, and marries another woman commits adultery."

The disciples said to Him, "If the relationship of the man with his wife is like this, it is better not to marry." But He said to them, "Not all men can accept this statement, but only those to whom it has been given. For there are eunuchs who were born that way from their mother's womb; and there are eunuchs who were made eunuchs by people; and there are also eunuchs who made themselves eunuchs for the sake of the kingdom of heaven. The one who is able to accept this, let him accept it."

— MATTHEW 19:1-12 NASB

One hundred fifty-four times in the New Testament, the word *oikos*[1] is mentioned, predominantly rendered as *household*. A formal definition reads: *all the persons forming one family; a household, stock; descendants of one; an inhabited house, home; any dwelling place belonging to a house or family, domestic, intimate.*

The Hebrew *abba* corresponds to the Greek *oikos* in that the housefather presides over a household, or a system or matrix, that engages all children, called sons. Just as the sons continue the greater household enterprise, so the *abba* designs, defines and designates the movement of the *oikos*.

An *oikos* is a spiritual ecosystem: a culture and Kingdom with economic, social, relational, and spiritual subsets that operate according to an appointed order of leadership, assigned by Jesus for the benefit of his metaphors building, body and bride. This matrix of Kingdom citizens, sons and inheritors are set into a Kingdom environment, where, from within, both the King and His leaders prepare and position inheritors of purpose.[2]

Mary's husband Joseph raised Jesus as his own, training him in the cultural norms of the Hebrew faith, and teaching the lad his trade. Creator-King matured Jesus as a faithful Son over His house,[3] inside the spiritual ecosystem known as an *oikos*. Jesus became intimately acquainted with Creator-King in this environment.

Ultimately, Jesus recognized the unseen King as His Father - His *Abba*. Jesus matured His Sonship through obedience. Jesus, known as Wisdom, continues the building, or maturing process causing expansion of the *oikos*, or household of God ... *whose house we are.*[4]

Jesus, as Wisdom, contributes prepared and positioned members of good standing toward the *oikos*. Matured sons rise as leaders, reflecting the five-fold service of Jesus in demonstration of function, namely: apostle, prophet, evangelist, pastor and teacher. Those who have matured to this stewarding trust in the scope of their function are placed in governmental assignment, not only to demonstrate the cultural example of behavior in Kingdom lifestyle, but to expand the King's estate. In other words, these matured members of the household of Creator-King are able to participate in the function of the *Ekklesia*, the jurisdictional body that brings the government of the King to the earth.

The greater citizenry of the Kingdom, called the commonwealth, is composed of the collective *oikos*. All commonwealth citizens are matured inside the most fundamental structure found in the universe: a *household set*.

A *household set* is embedded within the foundation of the architectural *blueprints of firsts* in Creator-King's original design. The first male and female were to be fruitful, multiply, and have dominion over the realm they had been assigned. A *household set* can be defined as a large organization of sons, daughters, and personnel, acting within the government of a central *abba*, the *housefather*. As such, each is a static nucleus, a dynamic governing body. This grouping of persons inside a household set maintains an economy with neighboring sets.

Abraham was just such a housefather. His leadership provided a central governmental command center. He instructed sons and personnel to the proper stewardship of livestock and his economy of great wealth. Abraham was responsible for the lives and the movement of those under his jurisdiction. This is the Biblical norm. The *oikos*, or household set concept, continues to function in the New

Covenant, according to the original design and pattern Creator-King intended.

The spiritual *oikos* of the Kingdom contains pillars of cultural norms. Situated atop the Kingdom attributes and components, these pillars are readily identified, and support the movement of the central governmental command center of Kingdom living. The first pillar of Kingdom culture is the covenant relationship of marriage.

Covenant Marriage

 From the beginning of creation, God created them male and female. For this reason a man shall leave his father and mother, and the two shall become one flesh; so they are no longer two, but one flesh.

— MARK 10:6 NASB

A marriage reflects the establishment of relational agreement in oneness. Integrity in this particular covenant provides a picture of a spiritual norm of geometric progression. Specifically, a marriage reveals the capacity of Creator-King to continue building His Kingdom of sons generationally. He maintains His covenant word of faithfulness to humanity, and expands His dominion over all the earth through the multiplication of offspring by His spiritual seed, the Word. Abraham was intersected in Ur, in part because he was of a disposition to command his children after him. He had a propensity to think and govern generationally.

Abraham was beleaguered by a character flaw of fear. Twice this flaw raised a test to Abraham. Twice Abraham utilized self-preservation over protecting his wife. Each encounter wherein he lied about his relationship with Sarah, he endangered his marriage covenant. Creator-King intervened on both occasions to keep His generational plan intact. The Biblical record gives no insight into how Abraham's repeated devalue of his wife - giving her away to a foreign ruler -

impacted their relationship. We do, however, see the impact of Sarah's insistent offer of her Egyptian servant Hagar as a partner to Abraham. The consequence of those actions resulted in the production of an heir, Ishmael, but not to Sarah's liking. Not only did her servant become haughty, Sarah experienced the loss of the intimate oneness of the marital covenant. Soon blame replaced trust, impacting the marriage and other members of the household set.

> *What God has joined together, no person is to separate.*

— MATTHEW 10:9 NASB

Covenant is an Eternal Force

Among the various types of covenant that exist, the marriage covenant is a direct reflection of Jesus' leadership among His brothers, the Body.[5] Just as Jesus holds His Body in regard, His deep abiding agreement of commitment is cherish-protected. Commitment is a building block of faithfulness. When a covenant is breached, it must be repaired, lest it prove to be a force of destruction. This applies to all covenant agreements, not simply the marital pledge.

Many passages of instruction are written within the Logos concerning the primary position of the union between man and woman. Notably, adultery is highlighted as the consummate foe of such a united oneness. Paul's letters to the regional *Ekklesia* in Ephesus,[6] Corinth,[7] and the injunction written to the believers in Rome highlight the spiritual implications of maintaining the fortitude of the blueprint.

Marriage is the epicenter from which the natural seed flows, providing humanity for Creator-King, partnering with Wisdom, to develop sons. The generational continuity remains intact.

In other words, marriage is the central load bearing pillar of the house that wisdom builds.

Let thy fountain be blessed: and rejoice with the wife of thy youth.

— PROVERBS 5:18 KJV

9

EXPANSION OF FAMILY

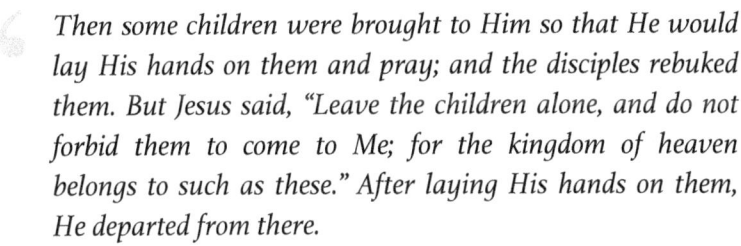

Then some children were brought to Him so that He would lay His hands on them and pray; and the disciples rebuked them. But Jesus said, "Leave the children alone, and do not forbid them to come to Me; for the kingdom of heaven belongs to such as these." After laying His hands on them, He departed from there.

— MATTHEW 19:14 NASB

There is a spiritual purpose to the expansion of family. Wisdom seeks to "gather a harvest of sons who are blameless and obedient." Without a strong foundation of family, the Kingdom will not expand in proper expression. Each household set is established with a covenant relationship of man and woman becoming one flesh. This union is to be fruitful, and multiply seed to the increase of a legacy government–a building; a house of sons and daughters.

Children are a gift of the Lord, The fruit of the womb is a reward. Like arrows in the hand of a warrior, So are the

children of one's youth. Blessed is the man whose quiver is full of them; They will not be ashamed When they speak with their enemies in the gate.

— PSALM 127:5 NASB

Family is the training environment that develops sons capable of leadership. Sons who are blameless and obedient and trained in upright leadership establish, maintain and expand the authority of the *abba* of the *oikos*, and ultimately the Kingdom. Additionally, expansion of the Kingdom requires leaders capable in service of enterprise function, and the art of war. Therefore, children are vital to the expansion of the household set and the *oikos* of the invisible Kingdom.

In addition, as a result of an ever expanding enterprise of stewardship, servants are often employed to labor alongside the burgeoning growth of an *oikos*. *He who pampers his slave from childhood will in the end find him to be a son* (Proverbs 29:21). The custom in ancient culture by which a slave became a permanent member of a household set, was demonstrated through the action of piercing his ear through at the doorpost of the home.

If your kinsman, a Hebrew man or woman, is sold to you, then he shall serve you six years, but in the seventh year you shall set him free. .... It shall come about if he says to you, 'I will not go out from you,' because he loves you and your household, since he fares well with you; then you shall take an awl and pierce it through his ear into the door, and he shall be your servant forever. Also you shall do likewise to your maidservant.

— DEUTERONOMY 15:12-16 NASB

At the heart of the concept of bond-servanthood was expansion-by-proximity and demonstration of commitment to the purpose of the central *abba*. A slave choosing to have his ear marked by piercing at the doorpost hearkened to the blood upon the doorpost at the passover, a defining moment in the history of the chosen people. The servant chose to be part of something greater than himself. His commitment was to the entire enterprise of home, family and economic gain. Choosing the *oikos* meant choosing the mission of the societal structure governed by the *abba*. The servant would now become a contributing member with full right of sonship, able to fulfill the duties and expressions of expansion.

Spiritual Offspring

> *Christ has been raised from the dead, the first fruits of those who are asleep. For since by a man death came, by a man also came the resurrection of the dead. For as in Adam all die, so also in Christ all will be made alive. But each in his own order: Christ the firstfruits, after that those who are Christ's at His coming, then comes the end, when He hands over the kingdom to our God and Father.*

— 1 CORINTHIANS 15:20-24 NASB

Jesus was sent to the earth first as seed, then as a first-fruits harvest. Creator-King continues to sow Him into the earth, through His function as the Word. The seed of the Word is scattered among the hearts of men. When the seed lands in a heart of good ground, new spiritual birth into the Kingdom occurs. The germination leads to the production of fruit, matured sonship, which is again harvested.

> *The soil produces crops by itself; first the stalk, then the head, then the mature grain in the head.*

— MARK 4:28 NASB

Through this cycle, Creator-King reaps a continual harvest of matured sons. As the ultimate *Abba*, the relational Creator-King shares His governing capacity with His sons. Through the process of discipline and training, the born-again children are raised as inheritors.

Every inheritor within an *oikos* is trained to do as their *abba* does in an apprenticeship of kingdom expression. Apprenticed individuals readily respond in submission to the *abba* and his matured representatives positioned among the *oikos*. The long season of continued training through obedience and maturation brings about the attainment of an inheritance, to become housefathers, or governors, themselves. The inheritance, a shared portion of assignment with the *abba*, expands the territory under the jurisdiction of the king. This is the purpose of the expansion of family.

Sons as Servants

Sons serve the house, in a great paradox to servanthood. Service to the intention of the *abba* stands as a vital expression of discipleship, the necessary training ground. It requires a specific attitude of heart, which is tested and tried in the field of training, during the course of duties of expansion. Service rendered to the *household set* is a stewardship which requires faithfulness.

It stands to reason that a son should rule, as a family member is considered more trustworthy than a laborer who is working for the family. The son has birthright, but position alone does not guarantee the preparation process will result in a statured inheritor. Maturity is a virtue that surpasses privilege. For example, Judah became prominent when his three elder brothers, Reuben, Simeon and Levi, forfeited their places in the hierarchy through a breach of covenant. In the event of disruption of the natural order, the *abba* may replace an errant or absent son with a wise servant. Likewise, if treated properly, a servant can become a son.

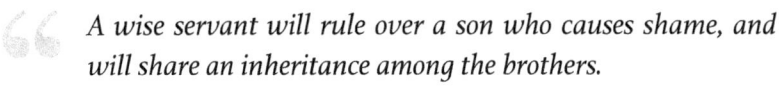

A wise servant will rule over a son who causes shame, and will share an inheritance among the brothers.

— PROVERBS 17:2 NKJV

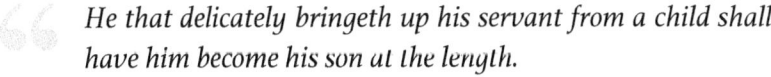

He that delicately bringeth up his servant from a child shall have him become his son at the length.

— PROVERBS 29:21 KJV

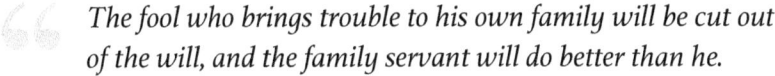

The fool who brings trouble to his own family will be cut out of the will, and the family servant will do better than he.

— PROVERBS 11:29 TPT

10

SONS IN RELATIONSHIP

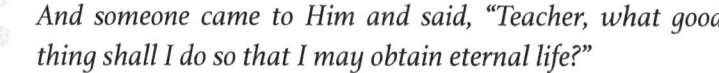

And someone came to Him and said, "Teacher, what good thing shall I do so that I may obtain eternal life?"

He said to him, "Why are you asking Me about what is good? There is only One who is good; but if you want to enter life, keep the commandments."

Then he said to Him, "Which ones?"

And Jesus said, "You shall not commit murder; You shall not commit adultery; You shall not steal; You shall not give false testimony; Honor your father and mother; and You shall love your neighbor as yourself."

The young man *said to Him, "All these I have kept; what am I still lacking?"

— MATTHEW 19:16 NASB

L uke, Mark, and Matthew all describe a man, a 'rich young ruler,' who encountered Jesus. In the original language, these terms identify him as a teenage youth of noble birth. In context of his culture, he would be considered an adult, now making seed, land, and livelihood decisions under the watchful eye of his father. Any missteps or mistakes, remedied with counsel; decisions of excellence, celebrated. As these important responsibilities were executed, the extension of the household purpose was expanded, and the wealthy young ruler contributed to the *oikos* as an inheritor.

Based upon his societal ability to influence through wealth and land ownership, the young man was likely a burgeoning leader among the Sanhedrin, the religious governing body of the Jewish nation. The Biblical account gives clues that he was of the party of the Pharisees. He demonstrated his political affiliation by communicating a strong sense of the law, and seeking to earn eternal life through a works-based system. He justified his maturity based on staunchly maintained adherence to the interpersonal laws of the Decalogue,[1] insisting the Torah had produced stability in his interpersonal relationships.

Jesus capitalized on his stated stability, recognizing it as a prerequisite for growth and maturation, by confronting the young ruler's social presence and power. Pointing to the vertical relationship with God as the primary source of upright horizontal relationships, Jesus made a demand for progress in his maturity. The rich youth recoiled from the direct affront to the righteous behavior mechanisms that had been instilled in him from his earliest memories. His hopes of Jesus' approval were dashed. This exchange exposes the third pillar of Kingdom culture: that of a son in relationship with others. Interpersonal relationships aid the creation of the fabric of culture. Relationships are a priority of the Kingdom.

The Natural and the Spiritual

Relationships in the Kingdom begin at the fountainhead of fathers. The context of Jesus' upbringing was expressed both in the natural, as a son of Joseph, and in the spiritual Kingdom, as the Son of God. The Scripture details Jesus, as a son in His Father's house, who learned obedience through the things He suffered. In both arenas, He had to mature in His sonship and accomplish the will of His Father.

The Greek describes five distinct phases that occur in the growth of a child. These terms in Greek are: *nepios, paidon, teknon, neaniskos,* and *huios.* Each phase of growth can be identified while looking through the lens of a home.

The first relationship in life is found between self and father, who provides a governmental structure supporting the culture of the house. The culture of the house is nurtured by the mother. The beginning point of this first relationship occurs at the *nepios,* or infant stage, indicating the child is an inheritor in position only. The parents' guidance provides a framework for growth through the *paidon* [toddler], and *teknon* [child] phases of life. Awareness of the father's presence, nature, preferences and behaviors develop. Also at these stages, sibling relationships are likely to be present, preparing a moral compass and staging integrity opportunities that will train for relations outside the immediate household set. Honor deepens and strengthens relationships, old and new, beginning with 'honor your mother and father.' Jesus encountered a teenaged youth - a *neaniskos,* wherein apprenticeship is exercised. The stature of a full grown son, a *huios,* becomes the point at which the son may fully represent the father.

As a representative of the father, the huios, or matured son, becomes an extension of a kingdom. A housefather matures sons and daughters to bring increase to a territory by reflecting the values of the *oikos.* Working together, the partnership for the livelihood of the *oikos* expands wealth and creates experiences. This produces a history passed down generationally through the telling of stories, becoming a legacy marked by *onoma*: the nature, character and authority of the housefather.

> *Tell your sons about it, And have your sons tell their sons,*
> *And their sons the next generation.*

— JOEL 1:3 NASB

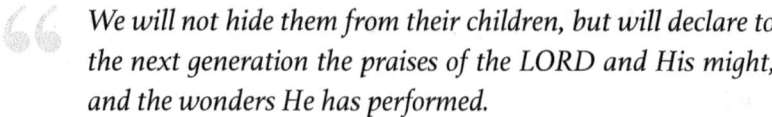

We will not hide them from their children, but will declare to the next generation the praises of the LORD and His might, and the wonders He has performed.

— PSALM 78:4 BSB

And it shall be when your son asks you in time to come, saying, 'What is this?' then you shall say to him, 'With a powerful hand the LORD brought us out of Egypt, from the house of slavery.

— EXODUS 13:14 NASB

11

OCCUPATION: STEWARDSHIP

Jesus said to him, "If you want to be complete, go and sell your possessions and give to the poor, and you will have treasure in heaven; and come, follow Me." But when the young man heard this statement, he went away grieving; for he was one who owned much property.

Jesus said to His disciples, "Truly I say to you, it will be hard for a rich person to enter the kingdom of heaven. And again I say to you, it is easier for a camel to go through the eye of a needle, than for a rich person to enter the kingdom of God." When the disciples heard this, they were very astonished and said, "Then who can be saved?" And looking at them, Jesus said to them, "With people this is impossible, but with God all things are possible."

Then Peter responded and said to Him, "Behold, we have left everything and followed You; what then will there be for us?"

— MATTHEW 19:21-27 NASB

> *If you have not been faithful in the use of that which is another's, who will give you that which is your own?*

— LUKE 16:12 NASB

Jesus, having startled the disciples and the youthful pharisee with His comments, framed possessions and ownership in a new light. Apprenticeship was not simply learning an occupation. The work assigned by the *abba* was about leadership. To apprentice meant one was being trained to assume leadership in that occupation. Leadership meant being a steward. To steward the occupation of the father as a possession not only meant to manage the resources, but also to engage in international trade. In this way, stewardship is directly attached to commerce.

The Greek term for stewardship is *oikonomia,* a compound word, merging *oikos*, a household, and *nomos*, a law. Defined as the careful use, control and management of the possessions of one that have been entrusted to another. The 'law of the house' is the instruction of the father as he prepares by equipping a function within a son that produces. The term is also used to refer to the responsible use of wealth and possessions by kingdom citizenry. Wealth was not about the favor of God, rather, it was an indicator of one's productive capacity while conducting jurisdiction in arenas of influence. Stewardship secured productivity for the generations to come, and positioned the *oikos* as a leader in commerce.

As a Biblical theme, stewardship is highlighted throughout the Word. Previously noted, Adam and Eve had been given a very specific task: to cultivate and tend the garden of Eden.[1] The function as husbandmen of the garden required them, as delegated authority, to have dominion over all aspects of the created realm.

Joseph proved to be a tremendous businessman, revealing his propensity for international trade as a birthright. The skill was handed down through his family line, great-grandfather, to grandfather, to father, empowered by the blessing of covenant cut between

Abraham and Creator-King. Joseph secured the skill of his birthright, as he stepped into the governmental position of second in command over the land of Egypt. He ultimately accumulated the surrounding real estate in Pharaoh's name.[2]

Daniel, taken captive to Babylon, found himself appointed as one of the top three commissioners in the country. His appointment meant he would steward the boundaries of the kingdom, according to the law of King Darius. His oversight included the economic well-being of that region.[3]

Stewards can be found moving collectively, in a collaborative effort, such as the seven chosen at Jerusalem[4] to wait on tables, providing service of daily food to the widows among the group. Stewardship extends beyond a certain field or trade, touching all possessions that come under the watchful eye of the individual assigned to a task. Stewardship as an occupation was the highest attainable skill.

Principled Occupation

Two main principles drive stewardship. They are: responsibility and accountability. Responsibility focuses on the role of an individual and how that person performs a specific task assigned to them, based on their gift mix or skill. Accountability is the ownership process of reporting results that have been produced by that specific task accomplished. Two passages of Scripture reflect these subtle differences, highlighting the importance of stewardship as a task, or, a job, an occupation that one must concern themselves with.

Responsibility

> *The Lord said, "Who then is the faithful and sensible steward, whom his master will put in charge of his servants, to give them their rations at the proper time? Blessed is that steward whom his master finds so doing when he comes.*

Truly I say to you that he will put him in charge of all his possessions. But if that steward says in his heart, 'My master will take a long time to come,' and he begins to beat the other servants, both men and women, and to eat and drink and get drunk; then the master of that steward will come on a day that he does not expect, and at an hour that he does not know, and will cut him in two, and assign him a place with the unbelievers. And that steward who knew his master's will and did not get ready or act in accordance with his will, will receive many blows, but the one who did not know it, and committed acts deserving of a beating, will receive only a few blows. From everyone who has been given much, much will be demanded; and to whom they entrusted much, of him they will ask all the more.

— LUKE 12:42-48 NASB

All action of responsibility begins with the king. The king owns one-hundred percent of the commodity or property He assigns or delegates to a steward, be it an individual or an *abba*. A steward will govern for the king as though the owner, only to release it back to the king at the close of the assignment. Therefore, what a steward does with the possession in his control is critical. To build responsibility, a steward must engage in the process of regarding what has been given to him as a trust by the king. The king has demonstrated it an honor to release a task to the hand of the steward, and once given, the king makes provision for wisdom to be attained by request. When a steward includes the king in the action of responsibility by asking for wisdom, he is empowered on how to proceed, allowing him to govern, grow, and maintain the item of charge.

As identified in the previous chapter, the maturity growth track of a son includes relationship development. When a son is put in position to steward an assigned task for the king, the process of responsibility shifts into high gear where others are concerned. Leadership requires relational finesse in sincerity and integrity. An awareness of others' overlapping assignments provides for training in honoring other types of gifting. The benefit and honor of others must lead the task or charge given. This provides the opportunity for integrity to operate, making the character of the steward exposed, and accessible by witnesses. Every action the steward takes will impact others.

The successful completion of various responsibilities leads the son-as-steward to expanded assignments. Then, built upon each previous success, continued cycles of expanding growth mature a steward to the place wherein he must account for his progress. The results-oriented focus of accountability always begins with mastered responsibility.

Accountability

"For it is just like a man about to go on a journey, who called his own servants and entrusted his possessions to them. To one he gave five talents, to another, two, and to another, one, each according to his own ability; and he went on his journey. The one who had received the five talents immediately went and did business with them, and earned five more talents. In the same way the one who had received the two talents earned two more. But he who received the one talent went away and dug a hole in the ground, and hid his master's money. "Now after a long time the master of those servants came and settled accounts with them. The one who had received the five talents came up and brought five more talents, saying, 'Master, you entrusted five talents to me. See, I have earned five more talents.' His master said to him, 'Well done, good and faithful steward. You were faithful with a few things, I will put you in charge of many things; enter the joy of your master.' "Also the one who had received the two talents came up and said, 'Master, you entrusted two*

talents to me. See, I have earned two more talents.' His master said to him, 'Well done, good and faithful steward. You were faithful with a few things, I will put you in charge of many things; enter the joy of your master.' "Now the one who had received the one talent also came up and said, 'Master, I knew you to be a hard man, reaping where you did not sow, and gathering where you did not scatter seed. And I was afraid, so I went away and hid your talent in the ground. See, you still have what is yours.' "But his master answered and said to him, 'You worthless, lazy servant! Did you know that I reap where I did not sow, and gather where I did not scatter seed? Then you ought to have put my money in the bank, and on my arrival I would have received my money back with interest. Therefore: take the talent away from him, and give it to the one who has the ten talents.' "For to everyone who has, more shall be given, and he will have an abundance; but from the one who does not have, even what he does have shall be taken away. And throw the worthless servant into the outer darkness; in that place there will be weeping and gnashing of teeth.

— MATTHEW 25:14-30 NASB

Mastered responsibility is a preparatory function, providing a platform for accountability to take shape in the life of a steward. Each time a responsibility is completed successfully, additional elements of the task can be added, until the full of the task procedure is known in all of its facets. Once each facet of a procedure is known and executed well, a report of results will provide a measurement for the king, defining the capacity of the steward to tend a matter. In this way, accountability is an ownership process, posturing a prepared steward to be positioned in increasingly greater function.

Results as a metric bring clarity to the king, allowing the trusted partnership to navigate new realms of expansion. The chief aim of all matured occupational stewardship is to expand the king's estate. The steward who is able to give account for the results he obtained while governing a possession of the king is promoted to a position of leadership, for which he was prepared and suited to fulfill.

The demonstration of accountability to Creator-King flows through His Kingdom leadership, the five-fold ministry. The five-fold function Kingdom leaders are matured sons, expanding the estate. They serve as an example, and as a plumb line, in that they have produced results for the King out of their function. They have demonstrated a capacity to steward the seed of the Word, the land of their assignment, and the livelihood that produces resources. As they bring account to the King, the expansion produced then becomes a part of the estate of the King.

Kingdom Leaders steward assignments and relationships. The relationships that develop in the Kingdom provide points of growth for the citizenry, giving opportunity for generations to mature.

A Job Well Done

The Kingdom lifestyle is one of stewardship. The responsible and accountable steward will present the results of his labor to the King as a husbandman. All citizenry, laboring alongside, engages in the stewardship process, to arrive at their purpose and destiny. Stewardship is the work of sons and daughters, that they might be mentored as they take up responsibilities and apply accountability. Accomplishing eternal destiny cannot be realized outside of Kingdom community. Therefore, the process of stewardship is performed in the social structure of the Kingdom, even within the *oikos*, to cooperatively release life to the whole. Every action is counted toward stewardship done well, or done poorly. A celebration of the partnership of stewardship done well ensues with provision made out of the result for a future investment.

Jesus dwells in the born again believer as His temple. The stewardship of the Kingdom of God is held within the Body. *Neither will they say, oh, look here, look there, it's within you.* (Luke 17:21) The seen has no choice but to be shaped by the unseen realm of Creator-King, built from the original blueprints and distinguished by the stewardship of the inheritors.

Occupational Guidelines

Throughout Scripture, the process and procedure of individual growth contributes to the whole of a community. The values held by a steward are identified as follows:

Stewardship is honorable.
One who tends the fig tree will eat its fruit, And one who cares for his master will be honored. PROVERBS 27:18 NASB

Stewards are entrusted and must be found faithful.
It is required of stewards that one be found trustworthy. 1 CORINTHIANS 4:1-2 NASB

Stewardship requires wisdom with gifts.
What do you have that you did not receive? And if you did receive it, why do you boast as if you had not received it? 1 CORINTHIANS 4:7 NASB

Stewards develop their gifts.
Do not neglect the spiritual gift within you, which was granted to you through words of prophecy with the laying on of hands by the council of elders. Take pains with these things; be absorbed in them, so that your progress will be evident to all. 1 TIMOTHY 4:14-15 NASB

Stewardship gifts are to benefit others.
As each one has received a special gift, employ it in serving one another as good stewards of the multifaceted grace of God. Whoever speaks is to do so as one who is speaking actual words of God; whoever serves is to do so as one who is serving by the strength which God supplies; so that in all things

God may be glorified through Jesus Christ, to whom belongs the glory and dominion forever and ever. Amen. 1 PETER 4:10-11 NASB

Stewards care for their body.
Your body is a temple of the Holy Spirit within you, whom you have from God, and that you are not your own? For you have been bought for a price: therefore glorify God in your body. 1 CORINTHIANS 6:19-20 NASB

Stewards use wisdom in caring for their entrusted possessions.
You are to remember the Lord your God, for it is He who is giving you power to make wealth, in order to confirm His covenant which He swore to your fathers, as it is this day. DEUTERONOMY 8:17-18 NASB

Stewardship of Land and Property

By Genesis extension, the blueprints governing the care-taking of creation have been handed down to humanity through the ages. The terra firma belongs to Creator-King. It is His to bestow as an inheritance. Therefore, land husbandry is an honorable occupation. Land has been assigned the task to produce. It cannot do any less. The fruit of the increase the land supplies is the stewardship responsibility of the Kingdom citizen as a resource earned.

> *For the Scripture says, "Do not muzzle an ox while it is treading out the grain," and, "The worker is worthy of his wages."*

— 1 TIMOTHY 5:18 BSB

Creator-King assigned land ownership in three capacities to His Covenant people: that of royal estate, serving the king and his constituents,[5] personal (and therefore private) jurisdiction,[6] and Levitical considerations,[7] for the care of the priesthood and tabernacle. Each capacity meant that the husbandman was required to care for property in a manner that would support the purpose for which the land was extended as a stewardship. Each endowment was provided with the expectation of increase, drawing forth valuable supply.

Whether king, priest, or *abba*, four arenas of care were to be tended: harvest left for the poor,[8] redemption law,[9] rule of fruit harvest,[10] and jubilee rest.[11] Minerals and metals mined from the earth were of custodial agency. The increase of the land was to be governed and managed for soil health and nutritive micro and macro nutrients, instead of bearing thorns and thistles.

The rich young ruler's wealth was tied to his ownership of land. While Scripture does not reveal that he mishandled his property, he received counsel which exposed his heart to the misplaced emphasis on the purpose of his wealth, and the product of his commitment.

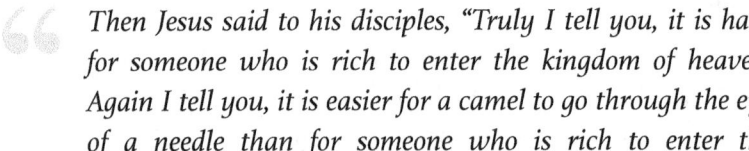

> *Then Jesus said to his disciples, "Truly I tell you, it is hard for someone who is rich to enter the kingdom of heaven. Again I tell you, it is easier for a camel to go through the eye of a needle than for someone who is rich to enter the kingdom of God."*

— MATTHEW 19:23-24 NASB

The Eye of the Needle

Much debate has occurred around the metaphor Jesus used with the upstart young man. While the eye of the needle appears to be hyperbole, expressing an impossible scenario, the camel described in the statement deserves consideration. The camel of ancient time was considered useful as a unit of trade, contributing to commerce in that day. Camel, *gamal* in Hebrew, was also used as a verb. In verb form, *gamal* meant *to invest;* or, *to nudge a fledgling toward productive maturity.* With this definition in mind, Jesus' instruction to *sell in order to obtain* gives a glimpse of how the principles of Kingdom economy function.

Stewardship is a partnership with the King for increase. The increase provides for those who tend the wealth, while maintaining the truth that the King owns it all. Stewardship is a son's apprenticeship to mature him to inherit.

Stewardship is a structural pillar of Kingdom culture.

> *If wealth increases, do not set your heart on it.*

— PSALM 62:10 NASB

12

KINGDOM ECONOMY & COMMERCE

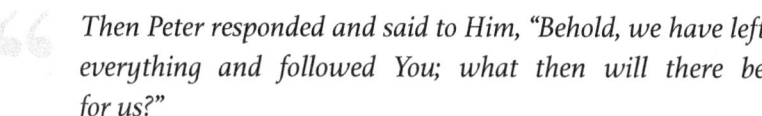

Then Peter responded and said to Him, "Behold, we have left everything and followed You; what then will there be for us?"

— MATTHEW 19:27 NASB

W here there is a steward, there is an economy; where there is an economy, there is a steward. The Kingdom pillar of economy and commerce is driven by creativity and investment.

Commerce has been a part of human existence from the beginning of time. Barter and trade, coming forth from an agrarian community gave way to monetary representation, such as the use of salt, or gold and silver by weight. Over time, metals would be smelted, forged, and imprinted with signet rings or imagery from the blacksmith's forge. Economy is expressed in a society through the use of measures and weights, balance and trade. What does the economy of the Kingdom look like? It can be described in several ways:

- Seedtime and Harvest
- Sowing and Reaping
- Giving and Receiving
- Land and the Livelihood
- Increase and Inheritance

Each descriptor brings forth a facet of process that impacts engagement with economic movement.

Creative Commerce

As an *abba* expands his *oikos*, he drives provision by way of creative commerce, employing barter, trade, and exchange as a means to move or receive goods. In ancient Israel, the land was described as flowing with milk and honey. Local trade included grains, olives, olive oil, grapes, wine, lentils, dried peas, beans, dried figs, dates and almonds. The remaining straw from grain harvest became marketable as valuable provender for oxen, sheep and goats. The livestock provided milk, cheese, and butter. All of these products became part of the economic viability of the house, and could be counted as trade-worthy to exchange for imported goods such as metals, cedar wood, textiles, and luxury products from other regions.

As a housefather, Abraham's skillful business dealings resulted in increase. However, when he chose to honor Creator-King by giving a portion of the spoils of war as an offering before the King-Priest Melchizedek, his economic efforts were given exponential growth through the power of Covenant. The result of his act of honor was the ever-increasing favor of God.

 Abraham was old, advanced in age; and the Lord had blessed Abraham in every way.

— GENESIS 24:1 NASB

Abraham's proclivity in international trade was present prior to his journey to Canaan. He was from the city of Ur, well known for its merchants, who carried out trade between the neighboring regions, primarily by caravan. Abraham journeyed away from the cosmopolitan city of trade, with its bustling economic system, to Haran, a known stop on an Assyrian trade route, to Canaan, wherein a society of people, equally proficient in international trade, lived. Successful international trade resulted in leisure and sport for these businessmen, yet economic exchange led to linguistic exchange, as people importing a foreign product would adopt the native term for the item. The process of exchanging language and goods provided for the development of synchronicity among people groups, bringing about the cultivation and maturing of society at large.

Upon the backs of numerous beasts of burden, notably the camel, caravans became trade route vehicles and therefore held great value in and of themselves. The camel, *gamal* in Hebrew, was considered an international unit of trade, much like a barrel of oil in today's economy. The presence of camels indicated the wealth of the merchant and his expanded economic reach into other nations. When the time came for Abraham to secure a wife for his son Isaac, he utilized the witness of his covenant with Creator-King, his wealth, in the form of camels. Camels carried the dowry back to his native country. It was but a fractional display of inheritance, and spoke to the spiritual and moral strength upon which Abraham's *oikos* was built.

> *The servant took ten camels from the camels of his master, and went out with a variety of good things of his master's in his hand; so he set out and went to Mesopotamia, to the city of Nahor. "I am Abraham's servant. The Lord has greatly blessed my master, so that he has become rich; and He has given him flocks and herds, and silver and gold, and servants and slave women, and camels and donkeys. Now my master's wife Sarah bore a son to my master in her old age, and he has given him all that he has.*

— GENESIS 24:10-12 NASB

Investment

Canaan, the land of purple,[1] would become the land of Abraham's destiny, and therefore required his investment. In addition to the creative commerce measures of trade, he secured the purchase of land in an agreement with the Hittite nation.[2] His purchase of the plot of land at the going merchant rate secured the whole of his business dealings with Canaan up to this point. The seed, the livelihood, and now the land merged into one realized and cohesive portfolio, received by faith that would define his life's work: he would direct his children and his *oikos* to keep the way of righteousness and justice. His generations to come, as inheritors, would expand the estate in a partnership assignment with Creator-King. The defining quality of the community would be that of the King, the one around whom all economy revolved, and from whom emanated all instructions by which the sons operated.

New Covenant Expression

Creative commerce defined the life and ministry of Jesus. Miraculous provisions marked His encounters with individuals. His creative miracles include the making of wine, the multiplication of bread and fish, and the restoration of sons to their *oikos*. As widows received their resurrected sons to life again, the sons were able to provide again for their household, and the greater population of individuals in their care. Jesus took great pains to articulate and demonstrate the industry of life in righteous capacity. He utilized justice and overturned corruption in regard to monetary dealings at the city gates and within the temple. His parables revealed that business was a vital part of a flourishing community. He encouraged responsibility and accountability, and chose to be an example of both attributes.

Matthew recorded the parable of the landowner, who employed laborers to work his ripened vineyard. Using wisdom and creativity, this particular *abba* provided a process that exposed the content of the heart of each set of hired men, for the purposes of maturing the men toward generosity. Likewise, Matthew recorded the parable of the talents to bring forward the concept of accountability as each steward matured the increase of investment. The capacity to reinvest the harvest seed to create a perpetual motion of expansion of inheritance provides the king his ever expanding estate of sons and dominion.

Taxation

Matthew gives a fresh perspective on the spiritual nature of economy within the Kingdom by introducing the concept of taxation. The king's sons, free from the requirement of taxation, nonetheless must conduct themselves in such a way so as not to bring reproach upon a the king while they are conducting business in his name. Matthew draws attention to this by describing the interaction among Jesus and Peter as they encounter the religious leaders:

> *Now when they came to Capernaum, those who collected the two-drachma tax came to Peter and said, "Does your teacher not pay the two-drachma tax?" He said, "Yes." And when he came into the house, Jesus spoke to him first, saying, "What do you think, Simon? From whom do the kings of the earth collect customs or poll-tax, from their sons or from strangers?" When Peter said, "From strangers," Jesus said to him, "Then the sons are exempt. However, so that we do not offend them, go to the sea and throw in a hook, and take the first fish that comes up; and when you open its mouth, you will find a stater. Take that and give it to them for you and Me."*

— MATTHEW 17:24-27 NASB

The religious 'tax collectors' were capitalizing on an Old Testament law that provided for the upkeep of the tabernacle in the wilderness–the tent of meeting. The practice remained, even after the physical temple was built. When Roman occupation began, the Jewish nation was allowed to continue their traditions of culture. The temple tax law stated that all men, age 20 or over, were to provide a "temple tax". Women, children, and the Levites were exempt from this tax, therefore, men of military service age were the ones called upon for the upkeep.

"When you take a census of the sons of Israel to count them, then each one of them shall give a ransom for himself to the Lord, when you count them, so that there will be no plague among them when you count them. This is what everyone who is counted shall give: half a shekel according to the shekel of the sanctuary (the shekel is twenty gerahs), half a shekel as a contribution to the Lord. Everyone who is counted, from twenty years old and over, shall give the contribution to the Lord. The rich shall not pay more, and the poor shall not pay less, than the half shekel, when you give the contribution to the Lord to make atonement for yourselves. And you shall take the atonement money from the sons of Israel and give it for the service of the tent of meeting, so that it may be a memorial for the sons of Israel before the Lord, to make atonement for yourselves."

— EXODUS 30:11-17 NASB

This tax associated health to census taking. Moses was instructed to take a census before the building of the tabernacle in the wilderness, presumably to regard each tribe by name. Elsewhere in Scripture, census taking for the purpose of assessing manpower was considered faulty. Numbering the multitudes was for the purpose of stewardship, and therefore used at strategic times in the history of the nation. Here, the acknowledgment of the individual made way for divine health to be provided for the whole.

As was common for the religious scribes, an over-zealous law-demanding premise drove their approach to Peter. No doubt they were attempting to capture Jesus in a law-breaking moment. Jesus initiated a query with Peter that placed the temple tax in a new framework: *'Who pays taxes for kingdom upkeep, Peter? Sons or strangers?'*[3]

The obvious answer, sons are not required to pay taxes, should have been apparent, as taxes are exacted from strangers in order to provide for the upkeep of a kingdom. Jesus, the Son of God was not required to pay, and Peter became increasingly aware of this fact. Earlier he had stated that Jesus was the Son of God when Jesus asked him, *"Who do people say that I am?"*[4] Therefore, Jesus' role as heir of God the Father brought about the exemption. Likewise, additional sons of the Kingdom are exempt. Kingdom citizens are not required to pay tax to the Kingdom of God as citizens are sons. The body of a son is the temple of God, and the tax for its upkeep has been paid as a ransom. Jesus had additional purpose in mind:

> *However, so that we do not offend them, go to the sea and throw in a hook, and take the first fish that comes up; and when you open its mouth, you will find a shekel. Take that and give it to them for you and Me.*

— MATTHEW 17:27 NASB

The phrase 'so that we do not offend,' is represented in Greek by the word *skandalizdo*. The English word 'scandal' is derived from this term. Engaging in scandal had the potential to shock the religious leaders unnecessarily. Surely, had Jesus recused Himself from this tax, it would have had a damaging effect on the effort to compel the leadership to yield to the Kingdom of God. Such a dismissive action would have overridden Jesus' mission, therefore He honored the directive in order to fulfill the Law. Utilizing Peter's learned trade, Jesus sent him to fish, expectant to see provision made abundant for both of them. Thus, the temple tax was paid in full.

Ultimately, Jesus, as Heir of the King, provided the ransom. The tax of the temple, as well as the payment for infirmity, the stripes He took upon His back,[5] was provided for all who believe. His sacrifice on the cross was more than sufficient to cover every Kingdom citizen. The children are truly free.

Creator-King owns all. His sons represent His ownership, even among strangers and foreigners in the world. Sons choose not to offend by employing the principle of honor to the King. In so doing, they support the infrastructure of His governmental expanse in the earth. The opportunity to impact and influence with dominion belongs to the heirs, who walk free of any spiritual taxation in the Kingdom.

The scripture, foreseeing that God would justify the heathen through faith, preached before the gospel unto Abraham, saying, In thee shall all nations be blessed.

— GALATIANS 3:8 KJV

13

KINGDOM AUTHORITY

 So Jesus said to them, "Assuredly I say to you, that in the regeneration, when the Son of Man sits on the throne of His glory, you who have followed Me will also sit on twelve thrones, judging the twelve tribes of Israel. And everyone who has left houses or brothers or sisters or father or mother or wife or children or lands, for My name's sake, shall receive a hundredfold, and inherit eternal life. But many who are first will be last, and the last first.

— MATTHEW 19:28-30 NASB

The sixth pillar of wisdom regarding culture is that of Kingdom authority. The result of having stewarded what belongs to the King ushered Jesus' audience into the expected end of their service: an inheritance of authority, a seat indicative of ruling and reigning with the Heir. Jesus described His ascent to the throne with clarity "... *when the Son of Man comes in His glory, and all the angels with Him, then He will sit on His glorious throne."* (Matthew 25:31)

A throne is a stately seat of rulership, the position upon which governmental authority rests. Often pictured in the mind's eye as an ornate chair that gives support to a regal magistrate, the Greek term *thronos* broadens the scope of modern day imagery. From the position of governmental rest, the opportunity to complete an organizational review, take inventory, and confirm control over the vast and complex economy is ambly accomplished. Jesus describes such activity, that of being seated, separating sheep from goat (reviewing and taking inventory) then issuing a verdict (confirming His control):

> *And all the nations will be gathered before Him; and He will separate them from one another, just as the shepherd separates the sheep from the goats; and He will put the sheep on His right, but the goats on the left. Then the King will say to those on His right, 'Come, you who are blessed of My Father, inherit the kingdom prepared for you from the foundation of the world."*

— MATTHEW 25:32-24 NASB

In a kingdom stabilized by a firm constitution of righteous rule, the king or governor settles down into his seat, and holds sway over all, as justice and legal authority. The Kingdom of God has co-regents; heirs who participate in the process of organizational review and the subsequent considerations:

> *"Because you have stood with me through all my trials and ordeals, I am promising you the kingdom that the Father has promised me. We will celebrate in this kingdom and you will feast with me at my table. And each of you will be given a throne, twelve thrones in all, and you will be made rulers on thrones to judge the tribes of Israel."*

— LUKE 22:30 TPT

The originating apostles, awarded the twelve thrones of judgment over Israel, carry the judicial capacity to rule alongside the King. However, all matured sons of the Kingdom reign with Christ, according to Ephesians 2:6: *But God ... made us alive together with Christ ... and raised us up with Him, and seated us with Him in the heavenly places in Christ Jesus.* From this position, seated with Him, the delegated authority of His rule flows from His citizenry, in a variety of arenas. Having been *seated with Christ* describes the positional aspect of stepping into council with God; in order to confer, and determine a course for a nation or a kingdom.[1] The delegated authority of the King provides for personal self-government, household government, regional, territorial, national, and so on. As a corporate expression, like unto a senate, the judicial, legislative body called the *Ekklesia* establishes and preserves the cultural norms based on the rule of the King.

I saw thrones, and they sat on them, and judgment was given to them.

— REVELATION 20:4-6 NASB

The Greek term for judge, *krinos*, means *to distinguish; to have the ability to see differences in order to express an opinion, judgment or assessment.* An emphasis is upon *the entire process leading up to an ultimate, carefully considered and complete assessment of a matter.* The evaluation is done in a painstaking examination by someone intimately knowledgeable of the issues at hand.

You have delegated to them rulership over all you have made, with everything under their authority, placing earth itself under the feet of your image-bearers. All the created order and every living thing of the earth, sky, and sea— the wildest beasts and all that move in the paths of the sea— everything is in submission to Adam's sons.

— PSALM 8:6-8 TPT

Interestingly, Jesus chose the city of Dan, established by the tribe of Dan which means 'to judge,' to reveal His ultimate purpose to the twelve. Now a Roman occupied city, named Caesarea Philippi, it had become a well-traveled crossroads. Suitable to the plethora of ethnic beatniks, they could find, nestled into the rock, a shrine to the god Pan.[2] The locals called it the Gates of Hades. From this geographical point, Jesus would retrieve the stolen birthright of the earth, and carry the government securely upon His shoulders.

The Covenant agreement, legal and binding, was ratified by His blood upon the Word of Creator-King. *Upon the revelation that I am the messiah, I will build My* [E]*kklesia.* (Matthew 16:18) The statement provided a focal point: that of an ultimate *Abba*, forming an *oikos*, wherein the householder would establish the behavioral and expressive law of the land. Since Jesus, Wisdom personified, reclaimed the right to rule, He would initiate the birthing, formation, and maturing of sons, that they might reproduce and expand the reach of His governmental rule.

The *Ekklesia*, therefore, would be the gathering of heads of *oikos*, merging into one council in a joint-sitting, able to confer, deliberate, and determine jointly produced directives among the peoples, asserting legislation according to the righteous rule, or law of the King. The gathering of these housefathers as self-governing assemblies of sons, servants, lands and livestock provided the opportunity for every voice to be heard in the greater-expressed Kingdom. In bringing the individual concerns to the council, the matters of life, including practical, political, and economic elements could be submitted for review and determination as to how to proceed. Thus, joint leadership provided for shepherding, rather than herding and dictating.

Speaking in the language of His day, Jesus mirrored the governmental process of the greco-roman period. An *ekklesia* was the political and governmental term[3] used for a group of people summoned and gathered to govern the affairs of a city or region. This was done by active participation in legislation; decreeing war; negotiating treaties or alliances; electing officials and more.

Tasked with the responsibility of numerous decisions concerning life and culture, the *ekklesia* would also select delegates who would go on to represent the nation in the areopagus.[4] Meetings would occur upon the rock of Ares, which by definition means "the god of war." The delegates functioned as a court to deliberate homicide, wounding and religious matters, as well as cases involving arson or the leading industrial product of commerce and trade: olive trees. After deliberating, they would send their determinations to the *ekklesia*, who would, at that juncture, arrive at a conclusion expressing the outcome, and hand down the ruling as final. Thus, a consensus of culture would be expressed throughout the collective *oikos*, and provide for a common thread of reflection: that of their King, whom they honored as worthy.

Securing The Gates

When Jesus reclaimed His name, I Am the Good Shepherd, He overturned the claim of Pan, who was worshiped at the gates of Hades, while simultaneously establishing that a joint-council form of leadership, the *Ekklesia*, would govern the Kingdom. He likewise established the format of leadership, that of the five fold function of His legislative body. These functions would provide the legal and jurisdictional framework of rule to be executed in the public square, namely, at the city gates. At the gates of cities, courts of justice were frequently held, contracts were written, and judicial decisions were rendered.

 The Lord is our judge; The Lord is our lawgiver; The Lord is our king!

— ISAIAH 33:22 NASB

14

WORSHIP THE KING

 But many who are first will be last; and the last, first.

— MATTHEW 19:30 NASB

Wisdom calls sons to live a lifestyle of worship to the King. Worship is a cultural pillar of the Kingdom. It requires a capacity to go low in honor and reverence to the One who created the pillars above and the pillars beneath the universe. Worship recognizes the Architect.

Worship is sound and sound is worship. Silence is sound and silence is worship. Everything that Creator-King marks with His Name is marked with sound. Sound is part of our identity.

The element of sound provides an indelible mark, a revealing of sons who are the sound of the King.

The Architect of oikos, the Creator-King, in His infinite wisdom, demonstrated a great Love by sending His only begotten Son. The Son surrendered His will, choosing to be willing and obedient unto the cross death in order to take back the dominion lost through the treasonous act of the first Adam. He allowed Himself to be matured by submission. He became the Heir of the Kingdom. As a first fruit offering, He gave His life that a harvest of sons might come in. Surrender and submission became His greatest act of worship to the Architect.

His action provided that He, the last–or, second–Adam, would now be first.

To Him, all Kingdom citizenry bow their knee in worship.

GLOSSARY

Chapter 2

1. **Basileus:** Greek noun for *governor, or lord over land. a prince; a commander; a leader of the people*
2. **Basilea:** Greek noun for *the land owned by the basileus, or king, considered the royal domain*
3. **Basis:** Greek noun for *foot, describing the function of walking, stepping, placing one's foot upon [the land]*
4. **Onoma**: *Greek term for name; the manifestation or revelation of someone's character, i.e. as distinguishing them from all others.*

Chapter 4

1. **Amud:** Hebrew for a. *great pillars, depicted by upright columns of smoke and fire.* b. *depicts scaffolding* c. *to take a stand; to cause to set up as erect; endure*
2. **Sod:** *Hebraic for secret, given through inspiration or revelation*

Chapter 6

1. **Pashat:** *hebraic for made plain, the obvious or surface meaning*
2. **Remez:** *Hebraic for hint, the deeper meaning, just beyond the literal*

Chapter 8

1. **Oikos:** *a family; a household*

Chapter 11

1. **Stewardship:** *the management, oversight, administration, of other's property*
2. **Oikonomia:** *A compound word comprised of two Greek words: oikos "a house" and nomos, "a law"*

Chapter 12

1. **Skandalizo:** *to put a stumbling block or impediment in the way, upon which another may trip and fall, metaphorically: to offend*

Chapter 13

1. **Thronos:** *Greek word for throne, meaning the position of governmental rest, the opportunity to complete an organizational review, take inventory, and confirm control over the vast and complex economy*
2. *Krinos:* *to distinguish; to have the ability to see differences in order to express an opinion, judgment or assessment*

3. **Ekklesia:** *the gathering of heads of oikos, merging into one council in a joint-sitting, able to confer, deliberate, and determine jointly produced directives among the peoples, asserting legislation according to the righteous rule, or law of the King*

ENDNOTES

Introduction

1. *History of the Brick Church and the Clapp Family*, Whitsett, William Thornton ©1925

1. The Invisible Kingdom

1. See *The Destiny Series, Identity*, by Rebecca D. Bennett, ©2021 for more on this principle.
2. Isaiah 14:13-14
3. 1 Peter 5:8
4. Philippians 2:8
5. Colossians 1:13
6. Isaiah 9:6
7. Philippians 3:20

2. The Creator-King

1. Genesis 1:26
2. *The Name Speaks, Doors Gates & Threshold Series Book 1* by Angela Broussard ©2021 See Chapter 2
3. *The Name Speaks, Doors Gates & Threshold Series Book 1* by Angela Broussard ©2021 See Chapter 1

3. The Creator-King As Architect

1. Strong's Concordance G2310: the foundations, beginnings, first principles
2. Strong's Concordance G2310: the foundations, beginnings, the first principles as referenced in the opening passage, Hebrews 11:9-10
3. *The Name Speaks, Doors Gates & Thresholds Series Book 1* by Angela Broussard ©2021. See Chapter 3.

4. Blueprints & Schematics

1. Strong's Concordance reference H5982, defined as column, upright; column of smoke or fire; standing on a platform
2. *Pentateuch* simply means "five books". In Greek, the Pentateuch (which Jews call the Torah) includes the books of Genesis, Exodus, Leviticus, Numbers, and Deuteronomy.
3. *The Name Speaks, Doors Gates & Thresholds Series Book 1* by Angela Broussard ©2021 Chapter 1.

5. Attributes of Kingdom

1. Dr. Myles Monroe presents a concise picture of the components of a kingdom. This chapter gives honor to his work, in a reflective capacity. For a fuller grasp on the subject, please see his entire treatise in *Rediscovering the Kingdom Expanded Edition: Ancient Hope for Our 21st Century World* ©2013
2. Strong's Concordance G4174, politeia: rights of citizenship; the administration of civil affairs.

6. Constitutional Stability

1. https://ancientegyptonline.co.uk/ptah/ accessed 6.30.2022
2. Moses experience is found in Exodus 2.
3. Exodus 3
4. *The Name Speaks, Doors Gates & Thresholds Book 1* by Angela Broussard ©2021, Chapter 1.
5. *The Name Speaks, Doors Gates & Thresholds Book 1* by Angela Broussard ©2021, Chapter 1.
6. Romans 2:14
7. Isaiah 9:6

8. Covenant Oneness In Marriage

1. Strong's Concordance G3624 and G3609
2. *God's Oikos: The Kingdom Matrix of God's Household,* Dr. Don Lynch ©2017
3. Hebrews 3:5-6
4. Hebrews 3:6
5. Ephesians 5:32
6. See Ephesians 5
7. See 1 Corinthians 7

10. Sons In Relationship

1. This is the name given in the Greek language to the ten commandments, listed in Exodus 20:3-17.

11. Occupation: Stewardship

1. Genesis 2:15
2. Genesis 39:4-6
3. Daniel 6:1-3
4. Acts 6:1-7
5. See 1 Samuel 8:14 and 1 Kings 21:1-2
6. See Joshua 14:6-13
7. See Joshua 21:1-41
8. See Leviticus 19:9-10 and Ruth 2:2-7
9. Leviticus 25:23
10. Leviticus 19:23-24
11. See Leviticus 25:2-4 and Exodus 23:11

12. Kingdom Economy & Commerce

1. https://www.jewishvirtuallibrary.org/land-of-canaan accessed June 2022
2. See Genesis 23
3. Matthew 17:25
4. Mark 8:27
5. See Isaiah 53:3 and 1 Peter 2:24

13. Kingdom Authority

1. Jeremiah 23:18
2. https://biblearchaeology.org/research/new-testament-era/3473-the-temple-of-caesar-augustus-at-caesarea-philippi accessed June 2022
3. https://www.britannica.com/topic/Ecclesia-ancient-Greek-assembly accessed June 2022
4. https://www.britannica.com/topic/Areopagus-Greek-council accessed June 2022

ABOUT THE AUTHOR

 Angela Broussard, in her professional capacity, serves as Director of Wells of SouthGate, a Five-Fold Training and Equipping Center on the Mississippi Gulf Coast. From this administrative leadership position, she functions in grace-flow as a Teacher, Prophetic Intercessor, as well as Strategic Co-Lead in Topographical Intercession Angela is a contributing and active member of the regional Ekklesia, apostolically led, with all five of the grace flows of Kingdom Leadership in operation.

Living as a Word-centric, Angela has impacted the lives of countless others through her empowering and Spirit-led teaching. Graced with a capacity to articulate the living status of the Word of God, students of the King have found themselves walking in ever-deepening measures of maturity, reflecting the nature, character, and authority of Christ.

Five children and nine grandchildren endow the Broussard family, as do the five donkeys, two horses, two dogs and numerous chickens. The combination leads to never-a-dull moment, with plenty of room for laughter to accompany them. The Lord's behest marked their decision to put down roots in the rudder of the nation.

Angela is commissioned and appointed in alignment with Network Ekklesia International, Wells of SouthGate, and Kingdom Harvest Alliance, Glory of Zion International Ministries. She is preparing to receive her Masters in Kingdom Leadership via Kingdom Leadership Institute, Jacksonville, FL.

Angela is available for ministry engagements, speaking appointments, workshops and conferences.

A Publishing Assist Company
Honor & Excellence as the seedbed of your written work

3Trees Publishing was born the result of the architectural build out of Wells of SouthGate. Following the blueprints for the region, 3Trees Publishing serves to reconnect creatives with their kingdom calling by supplying a framework of excellence for all printed work. This endeavor reintroduces and reconstitutes the original intent and design for the Spanish West Florida Territory and beyond.

Let the expression of your purpose be revealed as you prepare legacy for those who come after. For more information, use QR code to contact 3Trees.

THE NAME Speaks by Angela Broussard
His sound reverberates. Can you hear Him speak your name?

It is said that life is a journey and we are pilgrims on it. Discovering our strengths, weaknesses and opponents on the journey exposes the reality of the spiritual realm - and just how fortified it is. Each installment of Doors, Gates, and Thresholds will equip you to successfully navigate the unseen structural components of both the Kingdom of God and the Kingdom of darkness, leading you to victory upon victory. This, in turn, will empower the corporate expression of the Ekklesia, releasing power in greater measure, and you bring your victory to bear upon the whole.

The Name Speaks is the introduction to the Master Poet and His creation: you. Engage in the formation of your identity within the large context of the Kingdom, and come to know your vital role in service to the King. To learn more, use QR code to see books and tools by & to contact Author, Angela Broussard.

Designs x Laura
Let's manifest your vision

Designs x Laura is a brand and service for helping others find and interpret their vision. Whether you offer a product or service, are new or established in your field or maybe don't know what the next step is for you, you're covered!

For web design, graphic design and marketing services, please use QR code to view our portfolio, contact information or get started and book your consultation! If you don't see a specific need listed, feel free to reach out and our team will be happy to assist and discuss the innovation of your ideas.

The Destiny Series Books

STRATEGIC TRAINING TO DISCOVER YOU

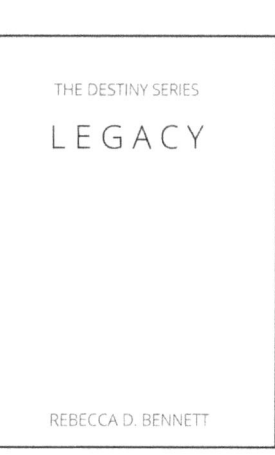

The Destiny Series is designed to help you discover the who and the why that you are. You are designed to become a great leader that God intended you to be, and you can reach your maximum potential in the ministry that the Lord Jesus gave every person (Matthew 28:19).

This dynamic and interactive series is available for individual or group study, as well as an author led course. To learn more, use QR code to view books now available by Author, Rebecca D. Bennett and much more.

Education

KLI GULF COAST

Kingdom Leadership Institute Gulf Coast

The leadership institute of choice prepares you for leadership in the Kingdom of God. The strategy of Kingdom Leadership Institute Gulf Coast is individualized. Your leadership training can begin at any level of spiritual and ministry maturity. We start where you are with what you do.

As one can function in any aspect of culture, once taught to function in kingdom culture, the Institute educates and prepares students for any arena of occupation. We honor kingdom leaders from every walk of life. Students come from many professions and occupations.

Partnered with KLI Jacksonville, our course intensives develop mature individuals to impact the current culture with Kingdom culture. Determine today to engage your life's work at the starting gate of Kingdom Leadership Institute Gulf Coast. For more information or to enroll, please use QR code or contact us via email at kligulfcoast@gmail.com.

Serve, Train, Empower

We Bring the Trainer to You.

- Community Advancement
- Business Training
- Leadership Development

Wells of SouthGate is a training, equipping, and activating center on the Mississippi Gulf Coast.

Our passion is to see each person matured to fulfill our God-given dreams and destiny, to become a flourishing, contributing member of their society. For more information, use QR code to visit the Wells of SouthGate website.

www.ingramcontent.com/pod-product-compliance
Lightning Source LLC
Chambersburg PA
CBHW060324130626
46553CB00003B/905